Counterfeit
Christianity

Counterfeit Christianity

The Persistence of Errors
in the Church

Roger E. Olson

Abingdon Press

Nashville

COUNTERFEIT CHRISTIANITY:
THE PERSISTENCE OF ERRORS IN THE CHURCH

Copyright © 2015 by Abingdon Press

This book is printed on acid-free paper.

Library of Congress Cataloging-in-Publication Data

Olson, Roger E.
    Counterfeit Christianity : the persistence of errors in the church / by Roger E. Olson.
      pages cm
    Includes bibliographical references.
    ISBN 978-1-4267-7229-0 (binding: acid-free paper) 1. Christian heresies. 2. Theology, Doctrinal. I. Title.
    BT1476.O47 2015
    273—dc23

                                                                            2015007535

15 16 17 18 19 20 21 22 23 24—10 9 8 7 6 5 4 3 2 1

MANUFACTURED IN THE UNITED STATES OF AMERICA

Dedicated to my Christian friends
Paul Frye and Greg Hildebrandt

Contents

Chapter 1
Understanding *Heresy*

Why Learn about Heresies?

Should you be reading a book about heresy? Some well-meaning Christians, including many pastors, would say no. "Put it down; go read about truth, not error." A popular sermon illustration says that when the United States Treasury Department (or Secret Service) teaches bank tellers how to identify counterfeit money they never show them counterfeit money; they only make them study real money so that they will recognize fake money as counterfeit by its contrast with the real. The point of the sermon illustration is to urge Christians to study truth, not heresy.

The first time I heard that illustration I doubted it. It just didn't seem likely to me. So I wrote a letter to the branch of the United States government charged with training bank tellers how to identify counterfeit money. I still have the responding letter in my files. The agent who responded denied the story and affirmed that they do, indeed, have bank tellers study counterfeit money. That's just common sense.

So how might the sermon illustration have started and why did it become so popular? (I've even seen it in introductions to books about Christian theology!)

I suspect many pastors would like their congregants to be more interested in studying the Bible and sound Christian doctrine than in learning about "cults." From the 1960s through the 1990s, America experienced a

1

wave of interest in so-called "cults and new religions"—spiritual movements alternative to traditional Christianity. Many Christians became obsessed with studying them. Some pastors and theologians were dismayed by the passion and fervor of cultists and anticultists and worried that people who were not well-grounded in the Christian faith could be easily swayed by persuasive rhetoric to join a heretical movement of non-Christian cult. ("Cult" was then used primarily for unorthodox, heretical religious teachings. Later it came to be used primarily for violent or abusive religious groups.)

While I understand that concern, I also worry that many Christians have little or no understanding of doctrines or beliefs that are contrary to historical, traditional Christianity. Those alternative doctrines easily slip in among Christians—sometimes merely through a misunderstanding of the Bible or sound doctrine and sometimes through infiltration—through teachers of false doctrines attempting to proselytize Christians to their way of thinking and believing.

Many Christians are gullible when it comes to being persuaded by smooth-talking purveyors of false doctrines. Others are simply not equipped to recognize false doctrines when they encounter them. Sometimes it's difficult to tell the difference between truth and error—especially for the non-theologian or non-biblical scholar.

This book is for those who would like to know what "heresy" means and why it is still a useful, even necessary, concept and how to discern between heresy and truth. But don't expect a litmus test! If it were that easy there would be no live heresies. Many contemporary Christians are concerned that their churches have become too pluralistic doctrinally. That is, they have adopted an "anything goes" approach to doctrine or dropped doctrine altogether. But what replaces sound doctrine is not a vacuum; it is chaos.

For those who may be getting nervous, because any talk about "heresy" makes people in our tolerance-driven society nervous, let me assure them that I am not a "heresy-hunter." I do not believe in doctrinal inquisitions. What I do believe in is discernment, something the Apostle Paul urged his first-century Christian readers to develop and practice. Doctrinal inquisitions and heresy trials are not necessary; Christian discernment is. Otherwise we, as Christians, have no common message to each other or to the world around us. We then are not a choir, singing the same message with different voices, but a cacophony, a confusion of sounds that just drive people away holding their ears.

Heresy depends on orthodoxy. Orthodoxy is theological, doctrinal correctness—right belief. Heresy is teaching (not just mistaken belief) that denies orthodoxy. In other words, heresy is serious, not minor, doctrinal error. It is, as will be explained throughout this book, error that strikes at the heart of the gospel of Jesus Christ. Every Christian denomination and church has some sense of orthodoxy whether they use that word or not. They all have some common belief and its ground, foundation, and structure is what C. S. Lewis called "mere Christianity" in his famous book by that title. Think of common Christian orthodoxy as "mere Christianity." I strongly recommend reading that book or one like it (another is G. K. Chesterton's *Orthodoxy*) to get a sense of what Christians have traditionally believed about God, Jesus Christ, the gospel, and salvation.

So, I agree with those who argue that it's more important for Christians to know what they should believe as followers of Jesus Christ and members of his church than what they shouldn't believe. On the other hand, we live in a world full of *counterfeit Christianities*—belief systems and doctrines that claim to be Christian and very seriously conflict with the gospel of Jesus Christ. Being able to recognize them as that, counterfeits of real Christianity, is important to Christian discipleship. *God cares what we believe about him.* Some beliefs about God seriously dishonor him by distorting his nature and what he has done for us in Jesus Christ. Or they inflate our human nature and ability to save ourselves, which is another way to dishonor God.

But also, studying false doctrines is a way of protecting the church. The church is the community of God's people and its health and well-being depends partly, at least, on believing in God rightly. Are we really worshipping God together if many of us have distorted ideas about who God is and what God has done for us and does in and among us? Again, the Apostle Paul urged first-century Christians to be of one mind—the mind of Christ. He didn't mean everyone had to think exactly the same thoughts; he meant all Christians should agree on basic truths about God and Jesus and salvation. Without sound doctrine, churches become little more than religious clubs.

Finally, studying heresies can help us understand and appreciate sound doctrine. One of my seminary professors was fond of saying to those who objected to studying heresies, "If studying these false teachings stings you into appreciating your own evangelical faith, then so be it! Be stung!" I can testify that studying heresies has never attracted me to them; it has always driven me back to mere Christianity, to orthodox Christianity, to traditional Christian doctrine. I have found all the real heresies (not everything someone calls heresy) unbiblical, illogical, and spiritually destructive.

Counterfeit Christianity?

Some people may bristle at the very idea of "counterfeit Christianity." We are very sensitive to intolerance, even to saying "you're wrong." It just doesn't seem polite. Only fundamentalists, those hard-core, rigid, narrow-minded Christians (and other religionists) talk about "counterfeit Christianity," right? I don't agree. I have never met a Christian who, when confronted with *some* version of Christianity, some so-called Christian belief, did not recoil in horror and think, if not say, *"That's not Christianity!"* During the 1930s, a group calling itself "German Christians" arose within the German Christian churches. They dedicated themselves to the Nazi party and ideology and to Hitler as a new messiah. This led to a "church struggle" in which another group, the Confessing Church, split away from the state-supported churches taken over by Nazis. Dietrich Bonhoeffer was a leader of the latter group. To this day, some Christians in the United States adhere to a White Supremacist ideology that promotes hatred of African-Americans and Jews.

Most Christians confronted with these phenomena will quickly say, "Oh, they're not *real* Christians." So not everything that claims to be Christian really is. But some Christians draw back from treating *any* belief as harmful in and of itself, so long as it doesn't result in violence or oppression. But, as one theologian has said, all heresy is cruel—in the sense that it turns people away from truth and toward illusion and distorts our relationship with God.

For nearly two millennia, Christians agreed that right belief is an important part of Christianity. They put different degrees of weight on it and often, unfortunately, went overboard persecuting those who were considered wrong. This is a large part of why many modern Christians (to say nothing of non-Christians!) tremble at the words *heresy* and *heretic*—because of the memory of people being drowned, burned at the stake, and tortured by defenders of orthodoxy. But not all defenders of Christian orthodoxy have conducted heresy-hunts or inquisitions; many have been loving and kind toward those they considered wrong in their beliefs even when they have had to correct them.

There are degrees of heresy. Surely racism in the name of Christ is worse than, say, belief in reincarnation. (The latter has traditionally been held as heresy by most Christian churches even though many Christians believe in it.) And there are many methods of dealing with heresy. Rarely is anyone physically harmed for teaching heresy—at least in the modern, Western world. However, gentle, loving, pastoral correction is also a way of dealing with heresies being taught by Christians. The latter is almost always the only way heresy is handled today, if it's handled at all.

The point is that there is such a thing as counterfeit Christianity and almost everyone who thinks about the matter knows it. Not everything that comes under the label *Christian* is compatible with the gospel of Jesus Christ. Certainly the "German Christians" were not real Christians and needed strong correction from pastor-theologians such as Bonhoeffer. When they would not allow themselves to be corrected and persisted in proclaiming Hitler a new messiah and Nazism as new gospel alongside, if not above, Jesus Christ and the Bible, real Christians had to separate from them and found the Confessing Church. The same could happen today—anywhere. Although most often counterfeit Christianity is a bit more difficult to identify and our contemporary American commitment to tolerance militates against any strong correction of it.

A basic presupposition of this book is that there is such a thing as counterfeit Christianity and that nearly every form of it has been around for a very long time. The heresies early Christians faced and dealt with are still challenging the gospel and Christian communities—from within and without. Live heresies are mostly ancient ones that just keep taking new forms.

The purpose of this book is to inform concerned Christians about these perennial heresies, counterfeit Christianities, so that they can practice discernment and correction among themselves—in a spirit of love. My goal is not to start heresy-hunts or inquisitions. It is only to help Christians know what major heresies are and what they believe and why they are counterfeits of truth.

If there is one major presupposition lying within this book it is that *if Christianity is compatible with anything and everything, it is nothing.* In other words, if Christianity is compatible with any and every belief, then it is meaningless. There is a cognitive content to Christianity; it includes a certain belief system, a worldview, and a perspective that includes doctrines. Serious departures from that undermine the integrity of Christianity and open the doors and the windows of the churches to all manner of confusion and declining discipleship.

Valid and Invalid Meanings of *Heresy*

Now is the time to clear up some common confusion about these terms. If you were to poll a hundred people coming out of ten different churches (to say nothing of a mall or other secular, public place) and ask them what *heresy* means, you would probably get fifty different answers. It's tempting to say heresy is an essentially contested concept. That's because, at least in a pluralistic social context without a state church or within a church or denomination without any enforced doctrinal orthodoxy, there is no standard or criterion for determining heresy. *Heresy depends on orthodoxy.* Where there's no orthodoxy, no theologically correct body of beliefs, heresy can hardly exist. At least not *formal heresy.* There can still be and always will be beliefs most people oppose. Try promoting socialism in any community in the Deep South of the United States! Even among people who have no religious orthodoxy you might hear charges of "heresy!" That's *informal heresy*—belief most people consider seriously wrong.

This book is about *formal heresy*—belief that is wrong by some agreed-upon standard. But in a pluralistic society such as the United States, there is no agreed-upon religious standard. What's heresy in one religious community isn't in another one. Still, I think we can talk about *formal heresy* in terms of *mere Christianity*. It would be belief that goes against, denies, or contradicts what Christians everywhere have always believed. It is doctrinal teaching that flatly contradicts the Great Tradition of biblical interpretation among Christians of all varieties—Eastern Orthodox, Roman Catholic, Protestant. Even most Protestant denominations and churches have *some* standard of belief that begins with the great teachings of ancient and Reformation Christianity—the deity and humanity of Jesus Christ (incarnation), the Trinity, original sin (that all humans for whatever reason stand in need of salvation), salvation by God's grace alone, the death and resurrection of Jesus Christ as necessary for salvation, the inspiration of the Bible, and so on. These, without much elaboration and addition, constitute *ecumenical Christian belief*—"mere Christianity."

If you were to gather together pastors and lay leaders of Eastern Orthodox, Roman Catholic, and various Protestant groups and ask them to begin listing their essential Christian beliefs, those are among ones that would appear at the top of most lists. Some lists would be longer than others. Typically, "fundamentalists" are those Christians of various denominations who tend to consider *all* their churches' beliefs as essential. Some would even include the "premillennial return of Jesus Christ" as an essential Christian belief. Some lists would be much shorter than others. Some, especially churches that consider themselves "moderate" or even "liberal," might have very short lists of essential Christian beliefs. A few might not consider any beliefs essential— until you asked them about racism, for example. But the majority would list the doctrines mentioned in the previous paragraph as essential and common (universal) Christian beliefs and at least say that they expect especially clergy to adhere to and teach them.

Doctrines that blatantly deny those common, essential Christian beliefs that go back into ancient Christianity, that are somehow or other rooted in the New Testament itself, and that were expressed in the early Christian creeds are the ones we are most concerned with here. Or, to be more precise, we are mostly concerned with their *denials*—heresies that reject them and are taught nevertheless, sometimes, among Christians.

But there's another form or degree of heresy besides that one. I'll call the ones I just described above "ecumenical heresies" because virtually all churches with roots in ancient Christianity or the Reformation recognize them as such. A second form is what I will call "denominational heresies." These are beliefs that contradict distinctive doctrines of particular denominations of Christians (or traditions—groups of denominations that believe alike).

For example, for a Catholic to believe and teach that Jesus Christ was not God incarnate, truly human and truly divine, is ecumenical heresy because virtually all Christians have always believed that—in spite of (as we will see) minority voices speaking out against it now and then. But for a Catholic to believe that Mary was born with original sin or died rather than being taken up into heaven in a kind of "translation" is also heresy. Those ideas about Mary are distinctive to Catholics, not Protestants, so they are only heresies *among Catholics*. Those are examples of what I call "denominational heresies" as opposed to "ecumenical heresies." Denominational heresies are not the main concern of this book. To begin to discuss all the denominational heresies would consume multiple volumes!

Another example of denominational heresy might help nail down the difference from ecumenical heresy. Baptists teach that only persons old enough to confess Christian faith for themselves should be baptized in water. It's called "believer baptism." Because Baptists do not believe infant baptism is "real baptism" (they consider it infant dedication with water) they will "rebaptize" (to use a non-Baptist term) persons who were baptized as infants.

For a Baptist to advocate and practice infant baptism would be heresy. For a Catholic or Lutheran to advocate and practice "rebaptism" would be heresy. (Catholics and Lutherans agree that infants should be baptized and that "rebaptizing" persons already baptized is seriously wrong.)

Every denomination has some written or unwritten distinctive doctrines and the denial of those constitutes what I am labeling "denominational heresy." But, of course, what's heresy in one denomination isn't in another!

If we were going to list all the ecumenical heresies, the subject of this book, the list would be relatively brief. But if we try to list all the denominational heresies, well, it would be difficult if not impossible to include them all in anything less than a library! There are, after all, well over three hundred major denominations in the United States and at least twelve hundred smaller ones!

So far, then, I've described *heresy* and two versions of it—"ecumenical" and "denominational." Now it's time to look at another important distinction—between "descriptive" and "prescriptive" uses of the word *heresy*.

When a person labels a doctrinal teaching as heresy he or she might be using the label descriptively or prescriptively or both. *Descriptive* means simply what it says—describing. When a person says, for example, that denial of the Trinity (usually a particular *way* of denying it) is a heresy, he or she might simply mean that most Christians have always considered it seriously wrong, destructive to the gospel, contradictory to Christian orthodoxy, and so on. He or she might *not* mean it *should* be considered heresy. The person saying it might not even be a Christian; he or she might be, for example, an atheist teaching about religion in a secular university (there are such). Clearly, such a person would not mean it *prescriptively*—that it *ought to be* a heresy.

Prescriptive means what it says—prescribing something as "ought to be believed." A person who says denial of the Trinity is a heresy might mean that Christians who deny the Trinity are, indeed, wrong and should be corrected.

Clearly, a person might mean that denial of the Trinity is a heresy in *both senses*—descriptive and prescriptive. It is highly unlikely that he or she would mean it only prescriptively, of course. A person who declares something a heresy prescriptively usually also means it descriptively. The only exception would be when a person is trying to convince others than his or her doctrinal opinion is more than mere opinion and ought to be taken on board, so to speak, as orthodoxy by a whole group of Christians as their orthodoxy (when it is not yet that).

These might seem like subtle distinctions, but they're not. Just think about it. Some beliefs are virtually commonly held as essential by all Christians—essential to authentic Christianity. Some beliefs are held to be essential for denominational affiliation by some group of Christians but not as essential for all Christians. But, of course, to complicate matters, some Christians make every belief, even their own quirky denominational ones, "essential to authentic Christianity." Those people are usually considered *sectarian*—a word religion scholars use for religious groups that consider themselves the only "true Christians."

The prescriptive/descriptive distinction is different but equally important. It doesn't have to do with essential versus denominational but with the intention of the speaker or writer labeling a belief as heresy. Does the person intend only to say that all or some Christians consider that belief heresy whether he or she does or not? That's descriptive. Does the person intend to say that he or she considers the belief heresy? That's prescriptive.

This latter distinction is often overlooked or simply unknown. I have had the experience of being invited to speak to a church group because I'm a historical theologian—someone who specializes in the history and development of Christian beliefs and practices. Sometimes when I say that a certain belief is heresy I mean that only descriptively but am taken as meaning it prescriptively, which then causes someone to object most strenuously.

Throughout this book I will be dealing mainly with *ecumenical heresies*—beliefs contrary to mere, common, orthodox Christianity as were agreed upon by faithful church leaders in early Christianity and also by the Protestant reformers. And I will be meaning heresy both descriptively and prescriptively.

Valid and Invalid Meanings of *Heretic*

Just as *heresy* has different meanings, so does *heretic*. The common assumption is that every person who believes in a heresy is automatically thereby a heretic. That's wrong. Of course, here we're up against such widespread use of a term that it's difficult to correct it. People commonly throw the label *heretic* at anyone they think is seriously mistaken about a doctrine or who holds an opinion contrary to their orthodoxy. That's an extremely informal use of heretic that makes it ultimately useless. That use of the term reduces it to an insult or a joke.

Actually, in historical-theological terms, at least for most Christian denominations, a person cannot be an "accidental heretic" or even an unwilling, unconscious heretic. Merely being wrong theologically does not make a person a heretic. It just means the person is wrong—perhaps unorthodox or "heterodox." The latter is a technical theological term for a belief or a person in conflict with orthodoxy. It's far less serious than "heretic" in the list of bad things a person might be (in terms of being in trouble with their faith community).

So what makes a person a true heretic? First, the person has to be *teaching* heresy to others. A person cannot be a heretic only in their own mind. They only become a heretic when they instruct other people in their heresy. Second, the person must *know* what they are teaching is heresy to their own faith community. In other words, a person cannot be a heretic totally outside of his or her faith community. Technically speaking, a person should never be called a heretic unless he or she fits the following: (1) is a member of a faith community and teaches against its orthodoxy, and (2) knows the doctrine he or she is teaching conflicts with the faith community's orthodoxy.

That must come as a surprise to many readers who are used to thinking many more people are heretics than actually are! It's not that easy to be a heretic.

I, for one, (and this is common practice among Christians educated in theology) do not label persons as heretics unless they know what they are teaching is against either ecumenical Christianity or their own denominational orthodoxy.

Now, a qualification is in order. Astute readers may already be thinking, "What about the person who doesn't belong to your faith community but denies basic, ecumenical, common Christian orthodoxy?" Yes, it's proper to call him a heretic if he knows that his teaching is contrary to basic, ecumenical, common Christian orthodoxy, even if his denomination tolerates it.

In this case, the "faith community" the person belongs to and whose orthodoxy she teaches against is *ecumenical Christianity*—the invisible, universal body of Christ, the church of the people of God throughout the ages. Of course, as there is no universal magisterium or church authority to govern that, such a person may very well be immune to correction. Calling her a heretic is, then, just a matter of opinion, even if educated opinion.

However, if a person belongs to a denomination or congregation that has specific beliefs, whether ecumenical or denominationally specific or both, she may be subject to correction and even discipline, possibly excommunication. But usually only if she is teaching against the orthodoxy recognized by the denomination. Some denominations, however, have completely given up on such church correction or discipline and allow anything to be taught. Or so they say. Their claim to be "free" and "pluralist" and "inclusive" is tested when someone speaks up in favor of racism or sexism or violence or hatred. Most denominations and congregations that claim to allow any belief draw the line somewhere.

All of that is to say that the label *heretic* is not necessarily inseparably attached to heresy. A person might very well believe in or even teach heresy out of ignorance. Once they are informed that what they are teaching is heresy and they continue believing or teaching it within that faith community, then they are a heretic. In other words, being a heretic is *always* presumptuous—never accidental or unconscious.

Examples of Ecumenical Heresies

One of the first Christian leaders to use the term *heresy* was Irenaeus, bishop of Lugdunum, what is now the city of Lyons in France (then called Gaul). He was born in Asia Minor (modern-day Turkey), which was then, in the second century, a hotbed of Christianity in the Roman Empire. His spiritual mentor in the Christian faith when he was a teenager was Polycarp, the bishop of Smyrna whose own mentor had been John, Jesus's youngest disciple and the reputed author of the Gospel of John and the book of Revelation. In other words, Irenaeus, who died during a horrible persecution of Christians by Romans in the early third century, was an important second-century link back to Jesus's own disciples.

Irenaeus was an emigrant from Smyrna to Lyons; he went there with a large group of Christians to help plant churches in Gaul. Eventually he became their bishop, or leader, and traveled between Lyons and Rome and other cities conferring with bishops about church matters. He was noted for being adept at helping settle controversies between Christians of differing opinions—especially about church government and structure.

11

Around 177, Irenaeus undertook to write a book against false teachings among Christians—especially in Rome. "All roads lead to Rome," and Christians from all over the empire traveled to Rome to promote their distinctive brands of Christianity. Some of them, Irenaeus believed, were false, counterfeit, and needed to be exposed as such. How did he know they were false? What gave him the authority to correct them? Ah, his connection through Polycarp (who was martyred in Smyrna in about 155 at a very old age) back to John.

There were self-appointed "Christian" teachers in Rome and elsewhere claiming to teach a more truly spiritual form of Christianity than the one being taught by Irenaeus and other bishops. They have come to be called *Gnostics*, which comes from a Greek word for "knowledge" or "wisdom." They claimed to have a higher Christian knowledge and to be more spiritually wise than the Christian leaders appointed by the apostles and then by the apostles' successors.

The doctrines of Gnosticism will be described in a later chapter, as will those of modern Gnosticism. Like most of the ancient heresies of Christianity, Gnosticism is alive and well in contemporary Christianity. Ireneaeus's main concern about them was that they denied the incarnation of God in Jesus; they denied that the man Jesus was God and human. To them it was impossible for God to be mingled with flesh and matter, so Jesus was either merely a human repository for a heavenly spirit-being sent from God *or* he was that heavenly spirit-being merely *appearing* to be human (docetism).

To correct the Gnostics and warn Christians away from their influence, Irenaeus wrote *Against Heresies* (in Latin *Adversus Haereses*) in five volumes. It constitutes the largest second-century Christian writing by a single author and the first Christian systematic theology (even though its main purpose was to refute heresies). Irenaeus did not invent the word *Haereses* for false teachings or counterfeit Christianity. He borrowed it from common Latin. It meant something like "independent thinking." But whereas independent thinking is valued today in the twenty-first century, it was generally viewed with suspicion in the ancient world. It meant going against tradition, which was considered truth. For Irenaeus, "Haereses" were not merely examples of independent thinking; they were teachings that flatly contradicted the teachings of the apostles about God, Jesus, and salvation.

Gnosticism was, throughout the second century, the "shadow" of apostolic Christianity. The various self-appointed Gnostic teachers claimed to be the purveyors of a secret gospel handed down by Jesus to an inner circle of disciples and by those few disciples to the Gnostics' teachers. They wrote their own gospels such as the Gospel of Thomas. Thousands of second-century Christians throughout the Roman Empire were seduced into Gnosticism. Irenaeus did much to set the record straight and expose the Gnostics as promoters of counterfeit Christianity. After him, they tended gradually to die away as a major influence among Christians, but some simply went "underground" and have always existed as the continuing shadow of orthodox Christianity under other names. As we will see, Gnosticism in permuted forms still exists in the twenty-first century.

Years ago I visited a friend's home. His grandfather had written a series of small booklets about the Christian faith and he showed them to me and suggested I read them. I tend to rise early in the morning, so one morning while staying with my friend and his family I sipped coffee and began reading the booklets. The first one talked about how before Constantine, the first Roman emperor to claim to be a Christian (around 311), Christians were all united in mind and spirit. All divisions arose after and as a result of Constantine's "conversion" to Christianity. I was then working on my PhD in historical theology and knew this to be false. I quietly put the booklet back on its shelf and said nothing to my friend who revered his grandfather. But I have found many Christians who labor under the same false impression.

The fact is that Christians in the Roman Empire during the second and third centuries (thus before Constantine) were deeply divided over doctrines and practices of the faith. Gnosticism was one cause of such division. Another was Montanus and his followers. He claimed to be a prophet who spoke directly from God and whose prophecies were equally authoritative with the teachings of the apostles (who were all dead by then but had left men like Irenaeus in charge of keeping their truth alive in the churches). Montanus taught, for example, that sex is sinful and true Christians should all be celibate. He drew his followers away from the churches led by bishops to a town in Asia Minor to await the coming of Jesus.

Another division among Christians was caused by a Roman Christian named Marcion who, during the middle of the second century taught that the Hebrew Bible, our Old Testament, was not inspired scripture and also rejected many of the writings of the apostles as too "Jewish." He taught that the world was created not by God but by an evil or demented "demiurge" (godlike being) and that the Yahweh of the Hebrew faith and Old Testament was not the Father of Jesus Christ. He proposed a canon (list) of inspired Christian writings that included only Luke, Acts, and Paul's epistles, some of which Marcion edited.

Also in Rome, around the beginning of the third century, was a Christian teacher named Praxeas who denied the Trinity. Or, to be more precise, he described the Trinity in a way that actually denied it. A North African Christian teacher named Tertullian wrote a book *Against Praxeas* (he also wrote against Marcion) to expose his teaching as serious error to be avoided by Christians. Praxeas's notion of the Trinity was picked up and repeated by (or independently arrived at) by other Christians throughout the Roman Empire and came to be called "Sabellianism" (after another heretic named Sabellius) and "Modalism." The essence of this common error was and still is (it exists today among Christians) that Father, Son and Holy Spirit are not distinct persons of the Godhead, the Trinity, but only "modes" or "manifestations" of the one person who is Yahweh, the creator and savior of the world. This became and remains one of the most common false views of God among Christians, but it was strenuously opposed, for very good reasons, by the bishops and fathers of early Christianity as well as by the Protestant reformers.

The point is simply that heresies, false doctrines, have always been around. The New Testament itself addresses them and, some scholars argue, is mostly written to correct them. The problem is, it's often difficult to tell who first-century promoters of heresies were or exactly what they were teaching. Sometimes the authors don't seem to know exactly, but they address truth in opposition to budding errors, counterfeits of truth. An example is the Apostle Paul's correspondence with the Christians at Corinth. His two epistles to the Corinthians deal much with doctrinal errors and harmful practices in that church. Some scholars believe Gnosticism was beginning to arise there; they call this early Gnosticism "proto-Gnosticism" (Gnosticism in embryo). For example, all the Gnostics of the second century denied the bodily resurrection of Jesus and our future bodily resurrection. Not because they didn't believe in miracles (like many modern people) but because they thought the body is the seat of sin and intrinsically evil (like matter itself). The whole of Paul's fifteenth chapter of 1 Corinthians is devoted to arguing for the bodily resurrection. In the background may have been a budding Gnosticism among those Christians. There are other hints of it in the New Testament itself.

Problematizing the Concept of Heresy

Many modern self-identified Christians reject the whole concept of heresy. To put it mildly, modernity, the culture stemming from the Enlightenment, has problematized the idea of heresy. This book will not address every objection to it; the purpose of this book is simply to inform interested people about heresies past and present. People who reject the whole concept of heresy will either not be interested or will criticize. I do want to address this issue briefly, however, so as not to leave readers in the dark about it.

There are two main reasons why some modern Christians reject the whole idea of heresy—at least as I am using it here (viz., counterfeit Christianity).

First, as mentioned before, many modern people are simply allergic to anything they perceive as intolerance; tolerance, especially of ideas, is almost a fetish or idol for modern, Western people. And, by tolerance, they don't mean just permitting people to have ideas; they often mean acknowledging all beliefs as equally true. This is called "relativism," although many people who embrace and promote tolerance don't acknowledge that their own belief is relativism because then it becomes self-refuting. Sheer relativism cannot be true if there's no absolute truth. So thinking people who affirm tolerance as an ideal usually only mean that nobody should be punished or excluded or sanctioned because of their beliefs.

Of course, one great benefit of the Enlightenment (although one could argue it has older roots among minority religious groups such as the Anabaptists) is freedom of religion from state control. Heretics are no longer tortured or burned (thank God).

However, many people leap from there to at least pretending to believe that all beliefs, especially religious or spiritual ones, should be accepted as equally true by everyone. But, of course, that would mean no religious or spiritual belief is universally true; it reduces them to subjectivity—private, personal opinion with no real claims to "true truth." The upshot of such an approach is that religion becomes at best "folk religion"—not true but merely a matter of personal preference.

Historically, Christianity makes truth claims. Not all of them have been true, of course, but to empty Christianity of truth claims is inevitably to destroy it. Without claims to truth for everyone, Christianity is no longer Christianity but "spirituality." That's the way some people want it, but then it is no longer really Christianity in any recognizable form.

Tolerance does not necessarily mean accepting every truth claim, even in religion, as equally true. And saying that some truth claims are mistaken, even seriously in error, is not intolerant.

The second reason why the concept of heresy has been problematized in modernity is the proliferation of Christian denominations and individualism. The great Enlightenment philosopher Immanuel Kant defined Enlightenment as "Think for yourself!" Most modern, Western people agree that all people should be free to think for themselves and not be told what to think or believe. Along with that has come a proliferation of religious sects and groups—many claiming to be Christian even though they often disagree with each other about very basic doctrines. Who's right? The temptation is to say it's all just opinion, or, at best a matter of private judgment. Very few societies any longer have a state church that has power to enforce belief on citizens. Even many Christian denominations lack any mechanism for deciding what their members ought to believe. Creeds and confessions of faith are largely forgotten or, even if they are recited in worship and learned in catechism, treated as optional—people are encouraged to pick and choose what parts of them to agree with.

Modernity has led to a situation where many people suppose religion to be private, individual, mainly about feelings or behavior (not doctrines), and where people start their own independent churches or denominations at the drop of a hat. What role does talk of heresy have in such a religious ecology? Many people would say none.

However, many people tire of Christianity being treated that way—as devoid of objective content and a kind of "free for all" in which anything goes and must always be accepted as Christian just because that's the label attached to it. Many people have learned that it's not uncommon for certain cults to promote themselves as Christian and hide the fact that their beliefs have nothing at all to do with historical Christianity. They have Jesus Christ among their pantheon of gods or heroes, which, they say, makes them "Christian." But many Christians have awakened to this tactic and become uncomfortable with the anarchy and chaos of "Christian" groups. It is for them that this book is written—to help them recognize the false from the true and gain a vision of Christianity as having belief content that actually excludes certain beliefs.

Without doubt heresy is a problematic concept in the modern, Western world. But I believe it's indispensable. Without it Christianity is reduced to a folk religion with no clear message.

Identifying and Dealing with Heresies

Many books have been written about how to identify heresies. The focus here will be on describing them more than on how to identify them. The major ones most Christians have always called out as heresies will be described—in their ancient and modern forms. But a few words about *why* these few errors have almost universally been considered dangerous to Christian faith are in order. Then I'll talk a little bit about how to handle heresies among Christians.

Each one of the heresies described in this book arose sometime in the first few centuries of Christian history—among Christians. Often, sincere, well-intentioned but misguided men (and a few women) thought they had discovered some truth the rest of the church was missing. But, most often, they were not themselves heirs of the apostles in terms of church leadership. Most often they were religious entrepreneurs who arose among Christians and began to condemn what the churches' leaders were teaching in the name of some special insight, new revelation, or higher wisdom. Occasionally they were leaders of churches, even bishops, but were out of step with the rest and persisted in promoting a doctrine the majority of bishops and presbyters (elders, pastors) found novel and inconsistent with the gospel handed down by the apostles and those they appointed.

But tradition was not the only criterion for determining what was heresy and what was truth. Although the canon (formal list) of New Testament books was not universally agreed on until the late fourth century, as early as the late second century most Christians throughout the Roman Empire agreed on certain gospels and epistles and other writings as truly apostolic and therefore authoritative. And the second-century church fathers such as Irenaeus and Tertullian (who lived and wrote into the third century) propounded lists of doctrines they were certain were apostolic. The heretics were those Christians who challenged this consensus about Christian belief in serious, fundamental ways. Ultimately they were judged to be promoting a "different gospel."

It's popular in some quarters to argue that there was no standard set of "orthodox" Christian beliefs until Constantine, who simply enforced the beliefs of bishops he liked. That's simply false. Constantine and his successors actually sided with heretics on many occasions! What had always been believed and taught by the apostles and their heirs was championed *against*

Constantine by courageous leaders such as Athanasius of Alexandria—exiled five times by Roman emperors for holding out for orthodoxy against compromises with heresies.

Some of the heretics were fine Christians otherwise; they were not all mad opponents of truth. In fact, every one of them claimed to love truth. They saw themselves as reformers of the churches. They quoted scripture to support their views. But, after much deliberation, the majority of church leaders decided (and the later Protestant reformers agreed) that their versions of Christian truth were ultimately destructive of the gospel. In most cases, the reasoning had to do with Jesus Christ and salvation. The heresies condemned as such by early Christians, before and after Constantine, were judged then and have been judged by most Christians ever since to change the truth about Jesus Christ and/or salvation into something else—different gospels.

All those early Christian heresies have continued to appear in different forms under different names throughout Christian history. All are still around, among Christians, in some forms. Throughout the era of "Christendom," the organic unity of church and empire that lasted from Emperor Theodosius (379–95) to the early nineteenth century (the Holy Roman Empire formally ended in 1806), governments often persecuted those perceived as heretics. For most of the nineteenth century and into the twenty-first century, persecution has virtually disappeared. A result has been that ancient ecumenical heresies have reappeared, coming up, as it were, from underground where they were hiding. People who had harbored heretical beliefs secretly became free to promote them openly and often even within Christian churches and seminaries. Or they founded alternative religious organizations ("sects" and "cults") based on one or more heresies.

What should be done about this? Well, of course, almost nobody (myself included!) wants to return to inquisitions. In most Western countries, especially the United States with total separation of church and state, heresies are free to flourish as they may. That's as it should be. But the question remains as to what Christians should do when they discover a heresy described in this book being taught or preached among them.

Some denominations and churches have processes for challenging heresies in their midst. Some do not and simply "roll with it," trusting God's Spirit to guide and lead the community to truth even through turbulent controversies. This book is not committed to any singular method of handling heresy, but I would suggest that a layperson who recognizes heresy being taught in his or her church ought to talk with the pastor about it. If that leads nowhere, then talk with the bishop or other administrative leader about it. If talking fails, sometimes a person must leave a church and find one where truth is respected and adhered to.

But what if you discover there's a new church in town that many people do not recognize is promoting heresy but you do recognize it? That happens fairly often. Some years ago, a group of Korean "Christians" began establishing churches in American cities and promoting a counterfeit form of Christianity based on the idea that a Korean prophet was the "Lord of the Second Advent." But, at least at first, they were very coy about it and presented themselves as traditional Christians with a new passion for the kingdom of God. I knew a number of Christian leaders who fell for their ruse and embraced them—until they discovered from more discerning Christians that the group held beliefs contrary to orthodox Christianity.

Some people go overboard "exposing" heresies. Whole organizations of conservative Christians devote inordinate amounts of time, money, and effort to that project and sometimes they sweep up into their net, to be exposed as heretical, groups that are nontraditional but not heretical. Caution is advised. Dialogue comes first. Before saying, "I disagree," make sure you can truly say, "I understand." Only then "expose" the heresy inherent in a new church or group with love to protect nondiscerning people, both Christians and non-Christians, from falling into it.

Bringing It Home

1. God cares about what we believe. What are three things essential to your Christian faith?

2. Discernment is a key spiritual gift. How can it help us examine what is true?

3. Find a copy of the Apostles' Creed and use it to discuss Christian beliefs and/or values. Do you agree with everything that the creed says? Where do some Christians disagree with it?

4. How might studying false doctrines help us protect the church and our witness? What might have happened to Christianity if early Christians had never come to a standard set of beliefs?

5. What would you label as "not Christian" if you saw it?

6. How might trying to be tolerant and inclusive make it difficult for others to know what we believe?

Understanding *Orthodoxy*

Heresy the "Mother of Orthodoxy?"

An old saying is that "heresy is the mother of orthodoxy." In other words, what we call orthodoxy, correct Christian belief, arose largely in response to the challenges of heresies. There is truth in that, and yet one has to be careful with the saying and the idea it expresses.

If the saying implies that there was no orthodoxy, no set of generally agreed upon Christian truths, until heresies and heretics confronted church leaders and then, for the first time, "correct Christian belief" was decided simply as a response to unwelcome teachings, then it is wrong. Any objective study of early Christian writings must conclude that Christians had an informal orthodoxy about God, Jesus Christ, and salvation before heresies arose. What we call orthodoxy was the result of working out the implicit beliefs of the early Christians, led by the apostles' heirs, in response to heresies and heretics. That's the truth in the saying.

Perhaps a simple analogy will illustrate the truth in the saying. Over the two and a half centuries of the United States' existence as a nation, the Constitution has been interpreted by courts, including especially the US Supreme Court. Often decisions about its meaning and application have come as a result of misinterpretations—what might be called "constitutional heresies." A common one is that the constitutional separation of church and state forbids public schools from teaching about religion or allowing religious student groups from forming and meeting on school property (e.g., "See You at the Pole" prayer meetings). The Supreme Court rightly determined that that is not what the Constitution means. But it only had to decide that as a result of certain separationist fanatics' attempts to stop students in public schools from studying religion, praying, and meeting for Bible study, for example.

Most constitutional scholars agree that the founding fathers would never have envisioned a time when students in public schools could not pray or study the Bible or learn about religion in social studies. So, the Supreme Court's decisions were not inventions of new constitutional truths; they were simply extrapolating the original meaning and applying it to a contemporary situation as forced by people misinterpreting the Constitution.

Of course, all analogies break down at some point. I am certainly not claiming that all Supreme Court decisions are correct. My illustration is only meant to show that something can be decided to have been true all along even when it never before had to be stated formally. That's true of much of what we call Christian orthodoxy.

The reason this is important is because some popular writers and even scholars claim that truths such as the Trinity were "invented" by Christian bishops under pressure from Constantine in the fourth century. That's a very serious misrepresentation of history. Anyone who reads second-century Christian writings such as the Apostolic Fathers (e.g., Justin Martyr and Theophilus of Antioch) and Tertullian cannot miss their emphasis on the triunity of God. And the second-century anti-Christian orator and writer Celsus clearly knew that Christians believed in the Trinity even if he misunderstood what they meant. The great Alexandrian church father Origen, who wrote hundreds of books of Christian theology and philosophy in the early third century, wrote much about the Trinity. It's simply absurd to claim that Christians did not believe in it before Constantine and the Council of Nicea in 325.

However, we need to make a distinction between this early, informal, and often implicit orthodoxy, what the vast majority of Christians believed that had not yet been formally spelled out and stated in a universal creed, and later, formal and explicit orthodoxy—the same truths spelled out and stated in universal creeds for all to confess. In between came the heresies. They challenged the informal orthodoxy so that the formal orthodoxy had to be formulated and carved in stone, as it were.

So there is some truth to the saying that heresy is the mother of orthodoxy, but its truth is limited and partial. Orthodoxy predated heresies, but heresies forced the church to make them explicit.

Some argue that orthodoxy changed during this process. That is, what the earliest Christians believed about the Godhead, Father, Son and Holy Spirit, was different from what the later church under Constantine and other Christian emperors promulgated. That's certainly open to discussion and debate. My conclusion as a church historian and historical theologian is that the substance was the same—only the wording changed. And the changed wording was necessary to protect the substance from misunderstanding and misinterpretation.

Orthodoxy Protects Mystery

One common misunderstanding of the formal, explicit orthodoxy of the universal creeds (Nicene of 325 and 381 and the Chalcedonian Definition of 451) is that their formulators were trying too hard to peer into mysteries of God that should be adored rather than understood. That is simply not true. It may be that they used language that is, today especially, obscure and confusing, sometimes borrowed from Greek philosophy. But their intentions were not to rationalize the mysteries of Christian faith by making them too easily understood. Their intentions were not to peer too deeply into God's being and ways to make them comprehensible to finite minds. Not at all. Rather, and this is extremely important, they were trying to protect mysteries of the faith from heresies that overrationalized them.

A great irony of especially modern thinking about ancient Christian theology is that the church fathers who thought about and defended Christian orthodoxy, and who formulated it into creeds, were rationalizing it away, emptying it of mystery. The irony is that they were doing exactly the opposite. It was without exception the heresies that were doing that! And a major catalyst for the formalizing of orthodoxy was to correct the rationalizing tendencies of the heretics. The heresies all made Christian faith too simple, too rational, too comprehensible to finite and fallen human thinking. Orthodoxy is not irrational but it is suprarational; it does not claim to explain the mysteries of the faith. It only claims to express the mysteries correctly and protect them from being reduced to finite dimensions of thought as if God were an object that could be studied and comprehended like something in nature.

This will be a major thesis and theme of this book—that Christian orthodoxy protects the great mysteries revealed in scripture from rationalization and that heresies tend to make what is revealed about God, Jesus Christ, and salvation in scripture too pictureable, too comprehensible, too simple. The result of all heresies is loss of transcendence—God's otherness. God is never "just like that"—referring to something created. There are created analogies of truths about God, of course, but heresies tend to make God, Jesus Christ, and salvation "just like" something observable in nature or in human experience.

All that is not to say that Christian truth should be incomprehensible, esoteric, or beyond all understanding. It is only to say that trying too hard to make it rational and comprehensible to the finite mind can distort it. That's what heresies do. They reduce the multidimensionality of revealed truth to one dimension; they drag God down into our "Flatland" (referring to the two dimensional world fantasized in the 1884 story "Flatland" by Edwin Abbott). We are like beings living in a two-dimensional reality whereas God is three or four dimensional. Like "flatlanders" in that two-dimensional world we cannot picture how God can, for example, be three persons and yet one being (Trinity). And yet that is what scripture reveals. Heresy attempts to confine God to our "flatland." Orthodoxy protects the multidimensionality of God in revelation, scripture, using language that sounds mysterious and even paradoxical but that is necessary in order to do justice to all that scripture says.

The Facets of Christian Orthodoxy: Early and Ancient

By now some readers will rightly be wondering what exactly *orthodoxy* includes in terms of necessary Christian beliefs. How detailed is it? Is Christian orthodoxy everything every church father and Protestant reformer believed? Is it a detailed systematic theology?

Let's be clear again. Here, in this book, we are examining what I called "ecumenical orthodoxy" in chapter 1. Others use different terms for it such as "mere Christianity" (C. S. Lewis) and "Nicene Christianity" (Christopher Seitz and others who wrote a book by that title). English evangelical pastor John Stott called it "Basic Christianity" in his very popular little book by that title. A difference between those books and the present one, though, is that here we will be studying orthodoxy by studying its denials—heresies.

I beg readers to keep in mind the difference between ecumenical orthodoxy and denominational orthodoxies. The former is singular, universal (agreed on by all three major branches of Christianity including most Protestant denominations in their traditional forms), and relatively simple. It constitutes the "essentials" in the old saying "in essentials unity, in nonessentials liberty, in all things charity (love)." Departure from it moves a person away from Christianity itself—in terms of Christianity's basic common beliefs about God, Jesus Christ, and salvation. Denominational orthodoxies are ecumenical orthodoxy *plus* doctrines important to specific Christian traditions but not essential to being Christian in terms of classical, historic Christian belief.

Another example may help make this distinction clear. The World Council of Churches, an ecumenical, cooperative body of hundreds of Christian churches around the world, requires member denominations to affirm that Jesus Christ is God and Savior. That's the core of ecumenical orthodoxy and has been since the second century if not before. But on secondary doctrines, outside that core, member churches disagree about many things. The Council includes Eastern Orthodox churches and Pentecostal churches. But some groups that call themselves Christian have been rejected because they do not believe and will not confess that Jesus Christ is God and Savior.

But, actually, ecumenical orthodoxy includes more than just "Jesus Christ is God and Savior." That's minimal orthodoxy. It's doubtful that the early Christian church fathers or major Protestant reformers would see it as sufficient. Necessary, yes. Sufficient, no.

So how do we go about identifying "ecumenical Christian orthodoxy?" One popular test proposed by an early Christian theologian named Vincent of Lérins has come to be known as the "Vincentian Canon": A Christian ought to believe (as orthodox) what has been believed by all Christians everywhere and always. Well, that sounds good, but as many critics point out, it's pretty hard to find any time or place where all Christians agreed on anything! Perhaps the canon should be changed to "most Christians"—especially Christians who were biblically committed and not accommodated to pagan or secular cultures. That is, there have always been people who called themselves Christians who knew little about the Bible or added to it philosophies and beliefs that contradicted it. I think that's what Vincent meant by "all Christians." (He actually said "everyone," so making that more specific begins with recognizing he meant "Christians" and I think it's justified to assume he meant biblically committed Christians not overly anxious to blend Christianity with pagan or secular philosophies.)

Of course, the Vincentian Canon raises the question, *What* has been believed by all (or even most) Christians everywhere and always?

One way to go about that is to examine the so-called "rules of faith" one finds in early Christian theologians (church fathers) such as Irenaeus and Tertullian. (Here *rule* means the same as *canon*—a measuring device, like a litmus test.) Facing off against groups and individuals they considered counterfeit Christians such as the Gnostics and Praxeus, both set forth brief statements of the teachings of the apostles handed down to them through people like Polycarp and embedded in the writings of the apostles (what later came to be called the New Testament).

One interesting thing about Irenaeus's and Tertullian's rules of faith is their strong similarity even though the two men did not know each other. Irenaeus wrote in Greek (even though most of his works survive in Latin translations) and was from Asian Minor where he was taught the Christian faith by Polycarp, a disciple of Jesus's disciple John. Tertullian wrote in Latin and lived in Carthage, a Roman city in North Africa. Strangely, perhaps, unless there was a general, ecumenical agreement among Christians about certain crucial doctrines, their rules of faith read much alike.

The reason for referring to Irenaeus and Tertullian as important is to counter the popular belief promoted by novelists and some scholars that there was no Christian orthodoxy before Constantine and later Christian emperors and their favored bishops created it in the fourth and fifth centuries. So we must look at Irenaeus's and Tertullian's rules of faith—written around 177 and 200 respectively (scholars date them slightly differently).

Irenaeus's rule of faith:

The Church, though dispersed throughout the whole world, even to the ends of the earth, has received from the apostles and their disciples this faith: [She believes] in one God, the Father Almighty, Maker of heaven, and earth, and the sea, and all things that are in them; and in one Christ Jesus, the Son of God, who became incarnate for our salvation; and in the Holy Spirit, who proclaimed through the prophets the dispensations of God, and the advents, and the birth from a virgin, and the passion, and the resurrection from the dead, and the ascension into heaven in the flesh of the beloved Christ Jesus, our Lord, and His [future] manifestation from heaven in the glory of the Father "to gather all things in one," and to raise up anew all flesh of the whole human race, in order that to Christ Jesus, our Lord, and God, and Saviour, and King, according to the will of the invisible Father, "every knee should bow, of things in heaven, and things in earth, and things under the earth, and that every tongue should confess" to Him, and that He should execute just judgment towards all; that He may send "spiritual wickednesses," and the angels who transgressed and became apostates, together with the ungodly, and unrighteous, and wicked, and profane among men, into everlasting fire; but may, in the exercise of His grace, confer immortality on the righteous, and holy, and those who have kept His commandments, and have persevered in His love, some from the beginning [of their Christian course], and others from [the date of] their repentance, and may surround them with everlasting glory.[1]

Tertullian's rule of faith:

Now, with regard to this rule of faith—that we may from this point acknowledge what it is which we defend—it is, you must know, that which prescribes the belief that there is one only God, and that He is none other than the Creator of the world, who produced all things out of nothing through His own Word, first of all sent forth; that this Word is called His Son, *and*, under the name of God, was seen "in diverse manners" by the patriarchs, heard at all times in the prophets, at last brought down by the Spirit and Power of the Father into the Virgin Mary, was made flesh in her womb, and, being born of her, went forth as Jesus Christ; thenceforth He preached the new law and the new promise of the kingdom of heaven, worked miracles; having been crucified, He rose again the third day; (then) having ascended into the heavens, He sat at the right hand of the Father; sent instead of Himself the Power of the Holy Ghost to lead such as believe; will come with glory to take the saints to the enjoyment of everlasting life and of the heavenly promises, and to condemn the wicked to everlasting fire, after the resurrection of both these classes shall have happened, together with the restoration of their flesh. This rule, as it will be proved, was taught by Christ, and raises amongst ourselves no other questions than those which heresies introduce, and which make men heretics.[2]

These very early Christian expressions of ecumenical orthodoxy give the lie to those modern novelists and (a few) scholars who claim doctrines such as the deity of Jesus Christ and Trinity were "invented" in the fourth century under pressure from Constantine and other half-Christian emperors. You will not see in them the language used to "nail down," as it were, the humanity and deity of Jesus Christ and the Trinity in the fourth century (viz., in the Nicene Creed and the writings of the orthodox church fathers), but the ingredients are all there. Between these rules of faith and the official creeds (including the fifth-century Chalcedonian Definition about the person of Jesus Christ) many heresies arose that denied the crucial doctrines expressed in them. That's why the fourth-century bishops felt it was necessary to formalize the rules of faith in ecumenical creeds—to protect what Christians had always believed and taught from counterfeit Christian teachings.

The Facets of Christian Orthodoxy— Later and Ancient

The third century of Christianity in the Roman Empire was a time of vast and terrible persecutions, but it was also a period of tremendous growth of the churches. However, not much was accomplished in the way of establishing and promoting ecumenical orthodoxy. Christian leaders were not permitted to meet; many of them were martyred or fled into hiding. Christian writings were burned, and even correspondence between Christian bishops was difficult. Heresies were simmering among Christians, but dealing with them took time and energy many Christians devoted to surviving.

In 311, Constantine became emperor and publicly credited Jesus Christ with his victory over his rivals. In 313, he signed the Edict of Milan that extended complete freedom to Christians. Christians were once again, as never before, actually, free to worship openly, build buildings (previous ones had mostly been destroyed under anti-Christian emperors), write letters and books, and travel to meet with each other. Most cities had bishops who had emerged as administrative and spiritual leaders over the presbyters—elders, priests. The second most important city in the empire was Alexandria, Egypt, and it was also the location of numerous Christian churches. Much Christian theology had emerged there and spread throughout the empire. Constantine was building a "new Rome" to be named after him—Constantinople. (It stood where present-day Istanbul stands in European Turkey.) Centers of Christianity such as Alexandria, Rome, and Antioch wanted their bishops and theologians to have influence in Constantinople because of the presence there of the first "Christian" emperor and his court.

But what became apparent soon after the Edict of Milan was that slightly different beliefs about Jesus Christ had arisen in various parts of the empire during the long persecutions of the preceding century.

The convoluted and often-troubling stories of those controversies among third- and fourth-century Christians over the person of Jesus Christ and the Trinity cannot detain us here. Suffice it to say that bishops and presbyters especially in the eastern, Greek-speaking half of the Roman Empire were dismayed to awaken to the fact that there were among them not only varieties of belief but outright heresies—very serious denials of the ancient Christian rules of faith and of scripture itself.

The century and a quarter from 325 to 451 is usually considered the formative era of formal ecumenical Christian orthodoxy. All the Protestant reformers of the sixteenth century who broke away from the medieval Catholic Church agreed with the main accomplishments of the councils that met and carved out correct Christian belief in extrabiblical but necessary language. The "jewel" of this process was the Nicene Creed, first written in 325 at the emperor-called Council of Nicea and revised in its final form in 381 at the also emperor-called Council of Constantinople (the first two ecumenical councils where all Christian bishops were either presented or invited).

The details of the 125 years of ancient ecumenical orthodoxy's formal formulation will unfold as we consider the heresies that led to it. For now, only the general outlines of what was decided then (and agreed to by the Protestant reformers and their faithful followers during the sixteenth and seventeenth centuries) can be described. That's so readers know what is meant by ecumenical orthodoxy—the basic doctrines of Christianity about which Eastern Orthodox, Roman Catholic, and most varieties of Protestants have always agreed.

In the year 325, several hundred Christian bishops gathered at a town in Asia Minor called Nicea. They came at the behest of Constantine to decide on a unified Christian doctrine about the person of Jesus Christ and ended up laying the foundation for a formal, orthodox doctrine of the Trinity as well. But that had to wait for its completion until a second ecumenical council in 381.

The bishops sat and discussed doctrine for days. Constantine was among them and occasionally intervened in the discussions to move them along. He did not, however, tell them what to decide. Constantine's exact role in the deliberations has been much debated, but there is no evidence that he controlled them. The vast majority of the bishops, excepting two or three, agreed relatively quickly on a way of expressing the relationship between Jesus and God the Father. They decided that they are "of the same substance" (*homoousion*). That is, whatever attributes the Father possesses as God are the Son's as well and that eternal, omnipotent Son of God, the Word, the Logos referred to in John 1, became one with us also. As we will see, there were other ways of expressing the relationship between Jesus and God and us, but they were declared wrong, heretical, by the bishops. That's when Constantine intervened and banished from their offices bishops who refused to go along with the creed that came to be known as the Nicene Creed. (In 381, it was revised to include an article about the Holy Spirit so it is technically called the Niceno-Constantinopolitan Creed.)

The first step in formalizing ecumenical orthodoxy, then, was a uniform decision that, according to Christian belief, Jesus is God incarnate—equal with the Father as to his deity and equal with us as to his humanity (yet without sin). Questions remained and had yet to be worked out. Confused bishops wondered whether this meant two Gods or perhaps one divine person with two countenances, roles, or manifestations. The next several decades were consumed with intense theological debate and reflection. In the end, when the next council met in 381, everyone agreed that "of the same substance" did *not* mean the Father and Son, Jesus, are two separate Gods or that God is one person with two faces or manifestations. In 381, the bishops thought to add the Holy Spirit to the Creed as a distinct person yet one in substance with Father and Son.

Many people get confused by all this. They think that either this was new thinking, perhaps imposed by politics and/or philosophy, or useless, unbiblical speculation by church leaders who had nothing better to do than peer into the mysteries of the Godhead. Neither assumption or conclusion is true. The bishops were simply responding to overly philosophical and speculative heresies and attempting to protect the mystery of what was always already believed by faithful Christians.

Here is the Creed that was finished in 381 at the Council of Constantinople and that has become the gold standard of ecumenical Christian orthodoxy for millions of Christians worldwide:

> We believe in one God, the Father Almighty, Maker of heaven and earth, and of all things visible and invisible; And in one Lord Jesus Christ, the Son of God, the Only-begotten, Begotten of the Father before all ages, Light

of Light, Very God of Very God, Begotten, not made; of one essence with the Father, by whom all things were made: Who for us men and for our salvation came down from heaven, and was incarnate of the Holy Spirit and the Virgin Mary, and was made man; And was crucified also for us under Pontius Pilate, and suffered and was buried; And the third day He rose again, according to the Scriptures; And ascended into heaven, and sits at the right hand of the Father; And He shall come again with glory to judge the living and the dead, Whose kingdom shall have no end. And we believe in the Holy Spirit, the Lord, and Giver of Life, Who proceeds from the Father, Who with the Father and the Son together is worshipped and glorified, Who spoke by the Prophets; And we believe in one, holy, catholic, and apostolic Church. We acknowledge one Baptism for the remission of sins. We look for the Resurrection of the dead, and the Life of the age to come.

This is the version of the Creed used by Eastern Christians; Western Christians later added the words "and the Son" (*filioque*) after "Who proceeds from the Father"—referring to the Holy Spirit. This was a major cause of the split between Eastern and Western (Catholic) Christians in 1054.

So what is the essence of this statement of Christian orthodoxy? To what does it boil down? Basically, it is a statement of the incarnation of God in Jesus Christ, that Jesus Christ is also God, "God too" (and "God two"), and that the Holy Spirit is also a person of God equal with the Father and Son. But! They are not three Gods because they share the same nature, substance, and essence. All have the same essential attributes of eternity, power, and glory.

As we will see, not all who call themselves Christians, both then and now, agree with this statement of Christian belief. For a variety of reasons and in different ways they reject it and are therefore considered heretics (insofar as they know they are rejecting Christian orthodoxy and persist in teaching their alternative view to others as "true Christianity").

After the Council of Constantinople, when everyone in the united church agreed about the deity of Christ and of the Holy Spirit and the Trinity, confusion arose among Christians about the relationship between the deity and humanity of Christ. In what sense was he both "truly God and truly human?" What does that mean and how should it be expressed?

Later chapters will unfold and explain these various "Christological heresies." Suffice it to say here that the bishops met again—twice—to settle these matters and say what all Christians should believe about Jesus Christ. The third ecumenical council was in Ephesus in 431. It condemned as heresy certain popular but distorted beliefs about Jesus Christ. The fourth ecumenical council met in Chalcedon, another suburb of Constantinople (near Nicea) in 451 to write a "Definition" of orthodox belief about the person of Jesus Christ. The Chalcedonian Definition is not really another creed alongside the Niceno-Constantinopolitan Creed (henceforth simply the Nicene Creed or even just "The Creed"). It was meant as a clarifying addendum to the Nicene Creed and it took on the same authority so that Christian groups and individuals who opposed it split away from the bishops.

So what did the Chalcedonian Definition say? The doctrine it promulgated is known as the "hypostatic union"—a technical term for belief that Jesus Christ was one unified person (not two) both human and divine. In other words, his person was the eternal Son of God, the second person of the Trinity, but he possessed both human and divine natures. This is a mystery and the bishops of Chalcedon knew it. Their whole point was to protect a mystery, not to dispel it.

Now let's step back from technical terminology and history for a moment and say in popular language (that scholars might not particularly like!) what these orthodox doctrines meant. The Nicene Creed means that Christians are to believe in a God who is "one *what* and three *whos*." The Chalcedonian Definition, hypostatic union, means that Christians are to believe that Jesus Christ is "one *who* and two *whats*."

The Chalcedonian Definition set up "four fences" around the mystery of the hypostatic union, the incarnation, to protect it from two main heresies that will be explained later. The Definition says that the two natures of Jesus Christ are "without division, without separation" and "without confusion, without change." In other words, in him, Jesus Christ, are two complete and distinct natures, one human (ours) and one divine (God's), and that these must not be regarded as separate, making him a double personality, or as mingled, making him a hybrid of deity and humanity (an impossibility given God's transcendence, wholly otherness than anything creaturely).

Another Facet of Ancient Orthodoxy: Salvation by Grace Alone

Throughout the first half of the fifth century, while Christian bishops were wrestling with the doctrine of the person of Jesus Christ and working out the hypostatic union formula, they were also dealing with controversies caused by heresies about sin and salvation—whether God's grace is absolutely necessary and whether humans are capable on their own, apart from God's supernatural grace, of living perfect lives of obedience or initiating a saving relationship with God.

Again, the heresies that caused this controversy won't detain us now; here we will discuss only the outcome—what the leaders of the churches, both East and West, decided is Christian orthodoxy about these matters. Readers need to be reminded that all the Protestant reformers and their followers agreed with what the bishops and other church leaders decided about this. The Reformation was *not* about whether salvation is by grace alone—that's ecumenical orthodoxy—but whether saving grace is activated by faith alone or by faith and "works of love." Catholic orthodoxy is that works of love are necessary for saving grace to finally to save a person (insofar as they are capable of works of love). Protestant orthodoxy is that salvation is by grace alone through faith alone without works. But both halves of Western Christianity agree that the gospel of Jesus Christ includes that good works alone do not merit salvation and that even the good works one does are products of God's grace.

The third ecumenical council, the Council of Ephesus in 431, dealt with several doctrinal issues including the person of Jesus Christ (foreshadowing the final resolution at the Council of Chalcedon in 451) and salvation, especially the relationship between grace and good works. In complete harmony with scripture (e.g., Eph 2:8) and earlier Christian teaching (e.g., Irenaeus, Tertullian, Origen, Athanasius, and other early church fathers), the council declared that good works alone cannot save a person; all are sinners and can be saved only by the grace of God through Jesus Christ. The Council did not deny the value of good works or the fact of free will; it only denied that anyone can be reconciled with God apart from God's supernatural grace.

Later, in 529, a synod of Western bishops at Orange (the Second Synod of Orange) condemned as heresy the idea that a sinner has the moral ability to initiate a saving relationship with God apart from God's grace. This will be explained in a later chapter. The heresy has come to be known in the annals of church history as "Semi-Pelagianism." (Pelagianism is the heresy that was condemned at Ephesus.) Semi-Pelagianism says that the human condition resulting from the "fall" (Adam's and Eve's original rebellion) is not all that serious; in spite of being born "fallen," sinners are capable of "exercising a good will toward God" on their own, apart from God's "prevenient grace."

(Prevenient grace is God's calling, convicting, illuminating, and enabling grace that overcomes the heart's bondage to sin and makes a sinner capable of repenting and trusting in Jesus Christ.)

Together, Ephesus and Orange and the testimony of the vast majority of the church fathers is that there is no possibility of any human being, other than Jesus Christ, living such a sinless life of obedience to God that he or she does not need God's supernatural grace—even to repent and believe.

Part of this last development of ecumenical orthodoxy, agreed to completely by the Protestant reformers and their heirs (including John Wesley), is the much debated and often rejected doctrine of "original sin." As with the concept of heresy itself, original sin has been problematized in modernity. Even many Christians reject it. But what does it mean? I suspect many who reject it do not even understand it. It never meant that human beings are evil or born with an evil nature in them. Church father Augustine spoke for most ancient Christians when he said that "the only evil thing is an evil will." There is no "sin nature" as such. Original sin has many interpretations and some of them are extreme and worthy of being questioned, if not rejected. But, basically, it means only that every human being (other than Jesus Christ and, for Catholics, Mary) is born "damaged goods" such that willful, rebellious, presumptuous disobedience to God is inevitable. Different denominations will explain when and how that "ticking time bomb" of original sin explodes into guilt, but "original sin" itself does not necessarily imply original guilt or even total depravity.

The great British Catholic lay theologian G. K. Chesterton famously quipped that original sin is the only empirically provable doctrine of the Christian faith. In other words, just look around you at others and inside yourself and you will see that, as the Bible says, all have sinned and fallen short of the glory of God (Rom 3:23). And "there is no righteous person, not even one" (Rom 3:10). However, the basis of the orthodox doctrine of original sin is not experience; it is the testimony of scripture and of all the church fathers and reformers.

Other Beliefs of Christian Orthodoxy

So far, then, we have discovered that ecumenical Christian orthodoxy includes: (1) the deity and humanity of the one person Jesus Christ (incarnation, hypostatic union), (2) the Trinity (God is one being, substance existing as three distinct persons), and (3) salvation is by grace alone and cannot be earned (even though good works are part of being a Christian).[3]

But what else is included in ecumenical Christian orthodoxy? These are the three great doctrines that bind all traditional Christians together and make them "Christian" in terms of belief. However, there are some other beliefs that virtually no one questioned until the modern age with the rise of secularity and naturalism (denial of miracles). Throughout the nineteenth and twentieth centuries, conservative, orthodox Christians of all varieties felt the need to defend certain doctrines early Christians and reformers never suspected any Christian would deny.

When we look back into scripture and ancient ecumenical Christianity and Reformation Christianity we can't help but notice certain common assumptions that never had to be formulated in the same way as the person of Jesus Christ, the Trinity, and salvation by grace alone. But they are implicit in the doctrinal statements and common worship and confession of Christians throughout the ages—until the rise of free-thinking liberal theology in the wake of the Enlightenment.

One is the reality of miracles including especially the resurrection of Jesus Christ. The "father of modern theology" Friedrich Schleiermacher (d. 1834) denied it. So did most "liberal" theologians of the twentieth century. Or, to be more precise, they "demythologized" it—meaning they interpreted it nonliterally as the "rise of faith" in the hearts of the disciples after Jesus died (while his body remained dead in the tomb). All conservative, traditional Christians have always held firmly to the bodily resurrection of Jesus. It would seem to be an essential part of the "package" of orthodox Christianity in terms of beliefs. Denial of it could safely be called heresy even though that's fairly common among liberal Protestants and a few Catholics.

Another item of ecumenical orthodoxy is that Jesus's death on the cross objectively reconciled God and humanity. If a person is saved it is due to the "atoning death" of Jesus. However, the ancient churches and councils never felt the need to spell out a particular theory of how Christ's death objectively reconciled God and humanity, making redemption possible. Theories have abounded in theological literature. But no one of them was "baptized" as the orthodox view by early Christian leaders. During the Protestant Reformation, belief that Jesus's death alone is the foundation of salvation was taken for granted; hardly anyone questioned it. Several theories of *how* Jesus's death reconciled God with humanity (and vice versa) appeared, but no one was universally agreed on as the one and necessary belief.

However, without going into details of the history of doctrines of the atonement (which literally means "reconciliation" and in theology refers to Christ's death reconciling God with humanity and vice versa) I can say with confidence that all traditional Christians both ancient and Reformation believed it was objective. In other words, the effect of Christ's death was not just an example of love that enables sinners to love God; it was also and more importantly a transaction of some kind, a sacrifice, a payment of a debt, a conquest of the forces of evil that kept God and humanity apart.

Other Christian beliefs were taken for granted by early Christians because virtually no Christians challenged them. The same could be said about the same implicit beliefs with regard to the Reformers—they may have disagreed about details of the doctrines but they all agreed on their essential truth. For example, that Jesus Christ will return to earth to raise the dead and judge all the living and dead and that Christians look forward to a new creation in the presence of God forever. Some modern, liberal Protestants have questioned this also (as they have the bodily resurrection), considering it mythological. They have "de-literalized" it, interpreting the second coming of Christ as the new presence of Christ in a Christian's personality upon conversion. But no Christian thought to deny the future return of Christ and the following new creation until some modern Christians succumbed to secularism and naturalism (denial of miracles or anything supernatural) and set out to reconstruct Christianity in radical ways.

Other items of implicit ecumenical orthodoxy include creation out of nothing, human beings as created in God's image and likeness, God's sovereignty over history (interpreted in different ways), and the church as the body of Christ (also interpreted in many different ways).

The Sources and Criteria of Christian Orthodoxy

Some readers may wonder from where ecumenical Christian orthodoxy comes and what it is based on. I've already mentioned the first four ecumenical church councils and several influential church fathers and theologians who wrote books to expound and defend common Christian beliefs. And I've mentioned that the main Protestant reformers wholeheartedly agreed with the early Christian leaders who formulated orthodoxy formally.

A key word in all this is *consensus*. Until the modern age when people calling themselves Christians openly denied basic Christian orthodoxy (as I have outlined it above) virtually all Christians of all types and tribes agreed on the doctrines of ecumenical orthodoxy. I say "virtually" because one can always find exceptions, but until modernity and the rise of liberal theology, those who disagreed with orthodox Christian doctrines were held to be heretics (insofar as they understood that they were disagreeing with orthodox Christianity). They were often mistreated, there's no doubt about that. In a notorious incident of particular cruelty, the heretic Michael Servetus was burned at the stake in the city of Geneva during the Reformation—for denying the Trinity. I have no desire to defend any persecution or prosecution of heretics. But, as I explained in chapter 1, the fact that churches and Christian leaders mistreated heretics does nothing to cancel the fact that heresy exists and needs to be exposed and opposed.

"Christian consensus," however, is not the ultimate foundation for Christian orthodoxy. It's one source and criterion for true belief, but it isn't the final or most basic one. That would be revelation, the Holy Spirit speaking through inspired scripture, the prophets and apostles and the writings they left for later generations and that God preserved for our inspiration, guidance, and teaching. The teachings of Christian orthodoxy are simply the church's attempts to be faithful to scripture.

Two issues immediately arise. One has to do with how we know scripture is God's written word and the other is the relationship between scripture and tradition.

As this isn't a book of apologetics (defending the faith) but an exposition of heresies, I must punt on the first question and simply say that, for Christians everywhere and always, scripture, however exactly understood, is considered God's inspired, written word to humanity. The early church fathers often referred to the "prophets and apostles"—meaning their writings in the Hebrew Bible and the apostles' Gospels and epistles plus Acts and Revelation. The formation of the Christian canon took time, but there was wide agreement on most of it long before the twenty-seven books of our New Testament were officially agreed on in the fourth century. Some Christians, myself included, believe the only "proof" of the authority of scripture as God's written word is what philosopher G. E. Lessing called "the Spirit and power."[4] Reformer John Calvin, in complete agreement with Martin Luther and others before and after, based our knowledge of scripture as God's Word and our understanding of its meaning on the "internal testimony of the Holy Spirit."[5] Defenders of the Bible have often appealed to "internal" and "external" evidences, proofs, of its unique inspiration to ground our Christian belief in the Bible. Of course, all such evidence and proofs fall short of absolute proof. One either sees the Bible as God's word or not.

A more important and pressing question for our purposes here is the relationship between scripture and tradition. Catholics, similarly to Eastern Orthodox Christians, view scripture and tradition as one united source of God's recorded revelation of truth. They refuse to separate them or place one over the other. For them, the ancient, ecumenical consensus I've been talking about as "Christian orthodoxy" is part of that revelation. Scripture is another part. They are two sides of one coin. Protestants generally (there are always some exceptions) disagree and place scripture over tradition. *Sola Scriptura* is the Protestant term for the primacy of scripture over all extrabiblical traditions.

Sola Scriptura does not mean, however, "Bible only" or even "Bible alone." It simply means the Bible is the foundation of true tradition; whatever a Christian ought to believe, whenever and however it is stated or by whom, is simply another way of saying what the Bible says. A traditional Protestant, for example, will say with Luther and Calvin and the radical reformers (e.g., Anabaptist) and John Wesley that the Niceno-Constantinopolitan Creed with its expression of the doctrine of the Trinity is true *because* it says in other words what scripture says. Its truth does not stand on its own legs; it stands on scripture's legs. *Should it ever turn out that something in the ancient Christian doctrinal consensus agreed to by the Protestant reformers is unbiblical, it will have to be changed or discarded.* Very few Protestants outside of liberal circles expect that ever to happen—unless "ecumenical orthodoxy" is made so detailed and comprehensive as to include everything the church fathers and reformers believed in common about anything. Then, of course, we are in real trouble because until Galileo in the seventeenth century everyone thought the sun revolved around the earth! That's not "ecumenical orthodoxy," though, because it is not taught in scripture and the church fathers and reformers did not make it a matter of dogma (official doctrine denial of which constitutes heresy).

Some Protestants seek a middle way between the Catholic view of scripture and tradition and the classical Protestant Sola Scriptura view. They insist that contemporary Christians, including Protestants, must *interpret* the Bible through the "lens," as it were, of the ancient Christian ecumenical consensus with which the Protestant reformers agreed. This *via media* view holds that scripture is "above" tradition but also that the Great Tradition of Christian orthodoxy must never be discarded, ignored, or set aside when studying the Bible for truth about God, Jesus Christ, salvation, and so on.

Like all via medias, middle ways, this one can incline toward either the Catholic view or the classical Protestant view. My belief is that scripture is our primary Christian source and norm for belief and that in all matters of doctrine scripture is the ultimate authority to which we appeal. As reconstructionist Jewish theologian Mordecai Kaplan said, "Tradition always gets a vote but never a veto."[6] Scripture gets veto power and every doctrine must prove itself on the basis of scripture. The Great Tradition gets a vote in a controversy over doctrine but never an absolute veto.

So, as we continue by discussing heresies, remember, please, that these are considered false *because* they contradict the gospel of God revealed in scripture, *not solely because* they are contrary to tradition. However, the Great Tradition of ecumenical orthodoxy votes solidly against them. That we should take seriously.

Bringing It Home

1. Reread the Nicene Creed. How do the beliefs that it outlines conform or not conform to your personal beliefs and the beliefs of your church?

2. Heresies make God too simple and too rational. How important is the mystery of God for you? Share a time that you experienced God? How did you/would you talk about it with others?

3. What is basic Christianity or "mere Christianity"? Discuss Christianity's three basic tenets: the person of Jesus Christ, the Trinity, and salvation by grace alone.

4. In your opinion, what is the relationship between grace and good works?

5. Do you understand the resurrection of Jesus as historical fact or in

a nonliteral way? Can a person be a Christian and not believe in the resurrection?

6. How do you understand the role of the Bible as faith's foundation? How does that understanding differ from the "Bible only" or the "Bible alone"? What is the role of the Bible in your life and daily faith practices?

Chapter 3

The Mother of All Heresies

Gnosticism

What Is Gnosticism?

Gnosticism is the perennial shadow side of New Testament, apostolic Christianity. It seems to have arisen immediately, with the rise of Christianity itself, and has always existed and sometimes flourished around the margins of Christianity. The second century was its heyday; after the Roman Empire became "Christian" it went underground. Today it is making a strong comeback labeled as "New Age" or "esoteric" Christianity.

Very few people have called themselves Gnostics; Gnosticism is a label invented by orthodox Christians to describe an alternative form of Christianity. During the twentieth century and into the twenty-first century, however, some people calling themselves Christians have attempted to revive ancient Gnosticism in new, modern dress and have identified it as such (and themselves as Gnostics). *Neo-Gnosticism* is a common term for all such groups. In 1997, esoteric New Age guru Elizabeth Clare Prophet ("Guru Ma") published a book entitled *Reincarnation: The Missing Link in Christianity*. There she and her daughter Erin L. Prophet argued that Gnosticism was true Christianity and had been wrongly oppressed and suppressed by orthodox churches. Her goal was to revive ancient Gnostic Christianity. (Most scholars agree that the ancient Gnostics did not believe in reincarnation, but neo-Gnostics believe they did.) A decade earlier, theologian Philip Lee published *Against the Protestant Gnostics*—decrying what he saw as latent Gnosticism in much of Protestantism.

"Gnosticism" is an essentially contested concept—at least among scholars. What exactly it is and was is very much debated. Some noted Christian scholars argue that there is some truth in Prophet's claim that ancient Gnosticism was true Christianity or at least that it was *as authentically Christian* as what people have come to think of as orthodox Christianity. Princeton University New Testament scholar Elaine Pagels built her reputation on that claim and sought to back it up with several highly regarded and widely read scholarly books. Her work brought new attention to the subject and led to a flurry of new books about it. Before that, however, an amazing discovery in the sands of Egypt renewed interest in Gnosticism and how to define it. In 1945, a whole library of Gnostic manuscripts was discovered at Nag Hammadi. It included many so-called "Gnostic gospels" that were previously only known by name via the anti-Gnostic writings of early orthodox Christians. Among them was the much-ballyhooed Gospel of Thomas. These writings were finally translated and published in one volume in the 1970s—shedding light on what ancient Gnostics believed in common and their diversity.

Much of what is known about Gnosticism comes from ancient church fathers and especially Irenaeus of Lyons, who died around 202. He was the bishop of Lyon in Gaul, France, and one of the first Christian theologians. He wrote five books *Against Heresies* that contain a great deal of information about and polemics against various second-century heretical Christian groups and teachers, including Gnostics. Irenaeus spent many years studying all the Gnostic sects that he could—many of whom were active in Rome where he traveled frequently. His *Against Heresies* spent thousands of words describing their teachings and criticizing, even ridiculing, them. Most scholars think his descriptions were fair and generally accurate.

Irenaeus recorded that some Gnostic leaders traced their special knowledge back to Simon the Magician mentioned in Acts 8, the man who attempted to buy the power of the Holy Spirit from the apostles. He also recorded that many Gnostic teachers claimed to possess secret teachings of Jesus given only to his inner circle of disciples and passed down from them to the Gnostic leaders. They would have been Peter, James, and John. The problem is, Irenaeus pointed out, that he learned the Christian faith from the martyr Polycarp who was a disciple of John. Surely, he argued, he would have at least heard of these secret teachings from Polycarp as he was very close to the youngest and last disciple of Jesus to die. He didn't. Irenaeus believed the special teachings of the Gnostics were invented by them either out of whole cloth or by putting together bits and pieces of Christianity, the mystery religions of the Roman Empire, and Greek philosophy.

Many people use the term *Gnosticism* very loosely. Here second-century Gnosticism will be the paragon and canon of all Gnosticism. Beliefs and teachings will be deemed Gnostic only to the extent they reflect distinctive themes of second-century Christian Gnosticism. Otherwise, the temptation to label too many things "Gnostic" becomes irresistible. For example, some people identify any religious belief that matter is limiting and that salvation involves escape from the material body and universe as Gnosticism. But real second-century Gnosticism went further; it identified matter as evil and the cause of sin and regarded salvation as escape from materiality by means of the discovery of one's own divinity.

So what did second-century Gnostics believe? What held the various "schools" of Gnosticism, each with its own teacher (Valentinus, Basilides, Cerinthus, et al.), together as a relatively identifiable movement?

First, Gnosticism was not just a set of doctrines; it was more an *ethos*—an attitude toward reality, especially time and matter or what some modern neo-Gnostics called "M.E.S.T."—matter, energy, space, and time. The attitude was disillusionment with history and a profound desire to escape time. It was also a negative attitude toward matter and a profound desire to escape it. Some scholars trace the beginnings of Gnosticism back to the failure of apostolic promises to materialize. Jesus did not come back as many expected. The envisioned kingdom of God on earth did not replace the Roman Empire and other oppressive structures. For Jewish Christians (whether there were ever non-Christian Gnostics is much debated), the fall of Jerusalem and destruction of the temple in 70 CE helped launch the Gnostic flight from history and matter into a purely escapist spirituality that came to denigrate time and matter as evil.

The other part of the Gnostic ethos was a tendency to divide all people, including Christians, into two groups—those especially spiritual people capable of higher knowledge and wisdom and those "physical ones" so deeply embedded in their bodies and the world that they could not understand the higher knowledge and wisdom (*gnosis*) and therefore were not candidates for recruitment into Gnostic circles. At first the Gnostics probably existed as

43

secret, exclusive cells within the Christian churches; later they split off and formed rival churches opposing those led by the bishops who were appointed by the apostles and their followers.

Thus, the Gnostic ethos was super-spiritual, otherworldly, even to the point of considering matter and time evil, as well as elitist, regarding non-Gnostic Christians and nonChristians as spiritually disabled.

The Heart of Gnosticism

This Gnostic ethos led to two crucial doctrines without which Gnosticism would not be Gnosticism. First, all Gnostics believed that sin arises from the body that is a "tomb" of the soul or spirit that is a "spark" of the divine or God that has forgotten its true divinity. Some ancient Gnostics have a phrase that in Greek was a play on two words—*soma sēma* or "body tomb." "The body is the tomb" would be a good English translation. The soul, the spark of God that is the core identity of a person, has somehow become entrapped in the tomb of the body and forgotten who and what it is. It sins because of this fallen condition, this evil materiality. Sin, then, is not freely chosen but a condition linked inextricably with embodiment. Salvation, then, must be liberation from embodiment.

Second, all Gnostics believed that salvation, liberation from embodiment, comes through the realization of the true divinity of the soul or spirit, which comes through receiving the hidden wisdom, secret knowledge, gnosis, of a Gnostic teacher. A Gnostic initiate would attach himself to a Gnostic teacher and become his disciple. Over time the initiate would be given increasing knowledge that was not for everyone. Eventually, through gaining the knowledge and using it, the initiate could, allegedly, experience escape from the sinful body and an ascent of the soul or spirit into purely spiritual realms leading up to the high God who is absolutely removed from this world.

Why second-century Christians rejected Gnosticism as heresy should be fairly obvious. First, building on Judaism and the Hebrew scriptures, Christians believed that God is the creator of everything and therefore nothing is in and of itself evil. The Gnostics had to posit an evil or demented god who created matter and time in order to keep the true God separate from evil. Second, the Gnostics had to blame sin not on the will of the sinner but on a condition over which she had no control—until becoming a Gnostic. Not repentance, then, but enlightenment became the path to salvation. According to apostolic, orthodox Christianity, sin is not a fate or condition but a choice for which people are responsible (even if they are born corrupted by Adam's sin). Third, the Gnostics had to deny the incarnation and resurrection—both Jesus's resurrection and our future resurrection. Jesus could not really have been human; he only appeared to be human. This is the heresy early Christians labeled "docetism" from the Greek word for *appearance*—that Jesus only appeared to be human but was not really and truly human. The Gnostics denied the resurrection of the body and emphasized the immortality of the soul or spirit.

But perhaps the worst heresy of Gnosticism, in the eyes of early and modern Christians, was and is the idea that the human soul or spirit is a "spark of God"—of the same substance as God and therefore divine. According to the biblical story and Christian teaching, the original sin was desire to be like God, to be God for ourselves—"idolatry of self." All sin stems from that. The Gnostics appealed to people's primordial desire to be God. Therefore early orthodox Christians considered them idolaters.

Gnostic Beliefs about Jesus Christ

The ancient Gnostics did not have a single, unified Christology (belief about Christ). However, they shared in common docetism—denial that Christ was truly human. To them, "Christ" was a "heavenly redeemer" sent by the true, high, purely spiritual God to teach the secret wisdom of humans' inner divinity to those spiritual people ready for such knowledge. This heavenly redeemer was not identical with God but also, like every soul or spirit, an offshoot of God. (Scholars call such ideas of semidivine mediators "emanations.") This spiritual redeemer being traveled down through the "aeons" (levels of spirit) between God and the world conquering those powers and forces ("archons") hostile to God and to Christ's mission. (According to most Gnostics there are fallen, hostile beings who oppose God's plans and purposes and attempt to thwart them. They were sometimes called "archons" but it's not improper to think of them as demons.) Christ fought his way through them and finally appeared on earth.

This is where Gnostics divided about Christ. For some of them, "Jesus" was the human appearance Christ took on so that he could teach humans how to travel out of their bodies, and thus out of sin, and back to their source in God. Christ was and is the purely spiritual heavenly redeemer who never was really born or died; he only appeared to be born and to die. His humanity, "Jesus," was all a charade. This is essential, original docetism, the Christological heresy most often associated with Gnosticism. Today, many Christians consider any denial of Jesus's true humanity as docetism whether it is attached to Gnosticism or not. One popular form of it is the saying that Jesus was "God with human skin on." In other words, his humanity was only skin deep; he wasn't really and truly human like us.

Much of the New Testament and second-century Christian literature aimed at affirming Jesus's true humanity. Some biblical scholars such as the German Walter Schmithals (d. 2009) believe that much of the New Testament was written to refute "proto-Gnosticism"—early Gnosticism in embryonic stage. For example, several times 1 John says that anyone who denies that Jesus Christ came in the flesh should be considered anathema (cast out). There must have been people among the early Christians denying that Christ came "in the flesh" (real humanity). Second-century Christian writings are full of affirmations of the real humanity of Jesus and castigations of people who deny it. Irenaeus built his whole doctrine of the "work of Christ" (atonement, reconciliation with God) on Jesus's true humanity as well as his true divinity. He had to be both truly human and truly divine to save the lost. This became standard, orthodox Christian doctrine and almost certainly always was implicitly if not explicitly.

A second Gnostic Christology divided Jesus Christ into two beings—one merely human (not at all divine or "heavenly") and one divine and heavenly (purely spiritual and not human). Schmithals and some other New Testament scholars point out that some second-century Gnostic groups required initiates to curse Jesus—as a way of demonstrating their spiritual wisdom. The point was to show that they knew and understood that "Christ" was not "Jesus" and vice versa. Jesus was merely a human vehicle of the heavenly redeemer Christ. Christ, purely spiritual, took over the body of Jesus until his death. When Jesus cried out "Father, *into your hands I entrust my life*" (Luke 23:46) he was saying, according to these Gnostics, that the Christ was leaving him. After all, this "Christ" could not be with him in death. So, according to this dualistic Gnostic Christology Jesus was unimportant except as a vehicle; the higher wisdom (gnosis) is that Christ is someone separate from Jesus even if he indwelt him for a time.

According to Schmithals and some others, this alone explains 1 Corinthians 12:3, which says that no one speaking by the Spirit of God can curse Jesus (or say "Jesus is cursed"). Why would Paul the apostle write that unless there were some in the Corinthian church (or influencing it) cursing Jesus? This hypothetical first-century Gnosticism is called proto-Gnosticism to distinguish it from full-blown second-century Gnosticism just as neo-Gnosticism distinguishes modern Gnosticism from its ancient prototype.

Gnosticism explains why second-century Christian literature, much of which is antiheretical, emphasizes Jesus's true and full humanity more than his deity. Not many Christians were denying his deity, at least not in the churches of the Roman Empire that were actively writing literature for Christians and to explain Christianity to outsiders. The issue dividing Christians was more his humanity than his deity. The incarnation of God in Christ was what was at stake and the main challenge was to Jesus's humanity.

Scattered throughout the New Testament are passages strongly affirming Jesus's true humanity. One needs only to mention, for example, Hebrews 4:14-15, which says that we have a high priest, Jesus, who has passed through the heavens (notice that it was not just "Christ" who did that but the man Jesus) and who was tempted just like we are yet without sin. All the Gnostics denied that the heavenly redeemer Christ could really be tempted because he was not attached to the material world but remained essentially free from it even as he appeared in it.

Some scholars think that the ancient Roman baptismal creed called the Apostles' Creed was formulated to keep Gnostics out of the churches. Nobody knows exactly where or when the Apostles' Creed was written but it almost certainly developed out of a second-century baptismal confession (a statement required of those being baptized into the church). The phrase "born of the virgin Mary, suffered under Pontius Pilate" ties Christ inextricably to history and matter. Gnostics could not say that about their "Christ." And the creed's opening line, "I believe in God the Father Almighty, maker of heaven and earth," may have been intended to refute Gnostic denials that God the Father made earth and exclude Gnostics who taught or believed in an evil or demented god who created it.

Christian Responses to Gnosticism

By the time Irenaeus wrote *Against Heresies*, Gnosticism was large and widely disseminated in the Roman Empire. In Rome alone there were several

Gnostic churches rivaling those founded by the apostles and their follow-ers. The idea of "catholic" arose largely to distinguish the latter from the former. *Catholic* meant those churches that shared in common apostolic origin and orthodox doctrine. A major Gnostic leader in Rome (but who traveled around the empire trying to proselytize Christians for his sect) was Valentinus. His followers were called Valentinians by others. Irenaeus chal-lenged Valentinus's claim to hold and teach secret doctrines of higher wisdom and knowledge passed down by Jesus to his inner circle and from them to him. To illustrate his argument against this common Gnostic claim, Irenaeus recounted a story told to him by Polycarp who had been the Apostle John's disciple and then became bishop of the Christians in Smyrna, a city in Asia Minor (Turkey). According to Polycarp, John was coming out of the city's public bath (the only place then to take a bath and a place for men to meet each other and have conversations) and saw the Gnostic Cerinthus there. He said, "Let us leave this place before the building falls down on us because the heretic Cerinthus is here!"[1] If the Gnostics knew and taught a secret spiritual wisdom communicated to them by Peter, James, and John, why would John have said such about Cerinthus, one of the first Gnostic teachers?

Irenaeus was the first Christian theologian as such. There were Christian writers after the apostles before him, and we possess and can read some of their writings, but he was the first Christian to write a large, detailed account of true Christian doctrine as opposed to false doctrines. In that way he be-came, as it were, the father of Christian orthodoxy—appealing to his intimate knowledge of the Apostle John's teaching, which he received in detail from Polycarp. He was also very familiar with the writings of the other apostles.

Irenaeus's argument against the Gnostics took three lines of attack. First, the one outlined above—that *if* the Gnostics carried on secret teachings from Jesus to an inner circle of his disciplines (including John) he, Irenaeus, would know it. Polycarp didn't and neither did he. There was no evidence, he ar-gued, that such existed. The Gnostic teachings were invented.

Second, Irenaeus exposed the Gnostic teachings as ridiculous. They in-cluded elaborate mythologies about the aeons and archons and their names. After all, that became how one was "saved"—by knowing and using the names of the spiritual beings blocking the path back to God or aiding people in their ascent out of the world of matter to reunion with God.

Third, Irenaeus argued that if Jesus was not human there is no salvation. The reason is that salvation depends on Jesus reversing the sin of Adam. This has become known as Irenaeus's "recapitulation theory" of Christ's reconciling work through his life and death. For Irenaeus, the Son of God, God the Son, had to take on humanity in order to undo what Adam did. Our human plight is due to Adam's disobedience; Christ had to undo that disobedience in the same "form" as Adam. For Irenaeus, Jesus's overcoming temptation was just as important as his obedient death on the cross. Every act of obedience was Jesus Christ reversing the disobedience of Adam for us. If we, by faith in him, enter into Jesus's new humanity, we leave behind the corruption of Adam's race and become "fully alive" (saved from death). According to Irenaeus, "The glory of God is man fully alive."[2] The Gnostics did not think one could be "fully alive" and be human. Salvation was leaving humanity behind and becoming purely spiritual. When Irenaeus said that the glory of God is "man fully alive," he meant to contradict the Gnostics.

For Irenaeus and all later catholic, orthodox Christians, the incarnation was essential to our salvation—not just to get God the Son onto the cross to die but also to join humanity with deity and reverse the curse of Adam's fall for all who would enter Christ through faith.

Theologian Lee, whose book *Against the Protestant Gnostics* was mentioned earlier, argues that too many modern Protestants have fallen into a Gnostic-like error not so much by denying the incarnation but by denying the physical nature of salvation. Protestants, he argues, have by and large spiritualized the gospel. Whether that's real Gnosticism is questionable, but Lee and many others have seen in modern spiritualized Christianity (including much hymnody that emphasizes immortality of souls over resurrection of bodies) echoes of ancient Gnosticism. For Lee and other critics, the reality of the incarnation should force us to realize how much God cares about matter and physicality. British theologian N. T. Wright has written several books emphasizing the redemption of this world in the future based on passages from Romans (e.g., second half of chapter 8) and the incarnation. This is to counter neo-Gnostic tendencies (mainly in Christian folk religion) to view future redemption as purely spiritual and not of the body or the earth.

Gnosticism after Gnosticism

Perhaps true Gnosticism should be limited to the second century. What came before it was proto-Gnosticism. What came after it was post-Gnosticism and what exists today is neo-Gnosticism. It all depends on how one defines *Gnosticism*. If it is defined nonhistorically as any religious denigration of time and matter, any purely spiritualized view of Christ and salvation, then it has always been around since the New Testament churches of the first century. But if it is defined historically it necessarily includes the heavenly redeemer myth. Most scholars tend to restrict true Gnosticism to that, so it was limited to the second century except where traces of that can be found "underground," as it were, in later Christianity. The temptation to label everything overly spiritualized as Gnosticism should be resisted. Lee's use of Gnosticism for much, if not most, modern Protestantism is an example of succumbing to that temptation.

The truth, or at least best approach, seems to be to talk about later echoes of Gnosticism and of Gnostic tendencies among Christians. Some have been stronger and clearer than others. Neo-Gnosticism is modern attempts to revive ancient Gnosticism with certain alterations such as belief in reincarnation (very common among modern neo-Gnostics).

So where did something like ancient Gnosticism appear after the second century? One clear example is the medieval Italian-French sect known as the Albigensians or Cathars that thrived in southern France and northern Italy in the twelfth and thirteenth centuries. Although their theology is murky and hotly debated by scholars, they seemed to believe matter is the source of all evil and that the material world, including bodies, was created not by the good God but by an evil or demented god. They became a major alternative to the Catholic church and built walled cities to defend themselves against crusades launched by Catholic forces against them. Eventually, their public existence was wiped out by a crusade but many believe they went underground and reappeared under different names in different locations in the Renaissance and later. The exact links between Gnosticism and Albigensians and later Gnostic-like groups are difficult to identify.

Perhaps the purest form of post-Gnosticism is a large and diverse movement known as "esoteric Christianity" that appeared in Europe during the Renaissance (fourteenth through the sixteenth centuries). Both the Renaissance and the Reformation opened the doors to new forms of Christianity including revivals of ancient sects blended with new ideas. Most of these post-Gnostic groups were eclectic. That is, they were anything but "pure Gnosticism" as described above (second-century Gnosticism). However, they echoed features of ancient Gnosticism and contrasted starkly with received catholic and orthodox Christianity (including Protestantism). Some scholars have called them an "alternative reality tradition in the West." They are lumped together as "esoteric Christians" because they all claimed to carry forth an ancient wisdom that was hidden except to a few. In the nineteenth and twentieth centuries, some of them claimed the time was ripe to make this ancient wisdom "exoteric"—public. Others combined exoteric with esoteric, opening some low levels of knowledge to seekers but holding back some for higher initiates only.

Perhaps the best-known and "purest" form of esoteric Christianity in the modern world is Rosicrucianism. Here, *Rosicrucianism* is not meant to designate any particular existing organization but a tradition older than they. There are several organized groups in Europe and North America that call themselves Rosicrucians, but Rosicrucianism is a theology or spiritual worldview not owned by any one group.

Rosicrucianism and Neo-Gnosticism

Neo-Gnosticism is virtually identical with Rosicrucianism. However, some neo-Gnostics do not label themselves Rosicrucians to avoid being identified with one of the organizations that uses that label. Similarly, people who call themselves Rosicrucians do not claim all neo-Gnostics as true Rosicrucians. Here *Rosicrucianism* will be used for an esoteric, neo-Gnostic worldview that echoes ancient Gnosticism in the purest form.

The beginnings of modern Rosicrucianism are shrouded in mystery— which is intentional. Rosicrucianism is supposed to be mysterious and somewhat secretive. Nowhere will you find a church sign that says "The Rosicrucians Meet Here." However, there is a Rosicrucian center with a large museum labeled as such in San Jose, California. Still, the vast majority of Rosicrucians do not announce themselves publicly. I once knew a Rosicrucian who would not actually admit to being one. How do Rosicrucians recruit people? Some Rosicrucian groups advertise in certain magazines. I have seen advertisements for Rosicrucian literature and correspondence courses in major news magazines. They display a symbol such as a pyramid with light rays emanating from its top. Underneath appears a series of questions about life before birth and life after death with strong hints about a "higher Self" one can ascend into. At the bottom one finds a post office box in either New York or California and an invitation to correspond. If one writes for the correspondence course, he or she will be gradually drawn into the group through stages, meeting with them only after the leaders have decided the person is spiritually "fit" to be a Rosicrucian.

Many such groups do not use the label Rosicrucian but also publish advertisements or post notices in public places (e.g., grocery store bulletin boards) inviting seekers to write to them or visit a website that contains very little concrete information but invites contact by mail or e-mail. The range of esoteric to exoteric is vast among these neo-Gnostic groups. Some are extremely secretive while others are almost totally open to those who approach. But all share a common disdain for making all their teachings public and all have levels of membership that lead to increasing knowledge of the "ancient wisdom."

Modern Rosicrucianism first appeared in London in 1717 when some neo-Gnostic Masons opened a Rosicrucian "temple" or Grand Lodge and invited seekers to visit and even join (after initiation). They claimed they were making slightly more exoteric an ancient teaching that appeared in Europe in the Middle Ages under the sign of a "Rosy Cross" and taught by a mystical figure named Christian Rosenkreutz ("Rosycross") and popularized by a physician named Robert Flood (or Fludd). Whether Rosicrucianism actually existed as an organized group before 1717, however, is uncertain. What is obvious, however, from Flood's writings, is that Rosicrucianism was revived Gnosticism. Early Rosicrucianism was designed to imitate Freemasonry or vice versa. Scholars debate that to this day. Some would argue that Freemasonry is exoteric Rosicrucianism and Rosicrucianism is esoteric Freemasonry. However, any connection between them disappeared long ago.

The key teaching of Rosicrucianism is the existence of the "higher Self"—a transcendent being of pure spiritual "light" that exists above every human being and is connected to his or her heart by a "silver cord." Rosicrucians differ among themselves about how literally to take the idea of the silver cord. The Gnostic element is that wrong attachment of the higher Self to the body; salvation comes through spiritual enlightenment about the divine nature of the higher Self and practices such as meditation that help the person live in his or her higher Self more than in the body. Some Rosicrucians believe in the possibility of out of body experiences. All believe in reincarnation, an idea added to ancient Gnosticism by most neo-Gnostics.

Rosicrucianism does not necessarily identify matter as evil, but it does tend to denigrate matter and the body as imprisoning of the higher Self.

Death brings the release of the higher Self from the body (the silver cord breaks) into spiritual realms and a process of spiritual evolution that includes several reincarnations but eventual reunion with God through perfect enlightenment. Rosicrucians view Christ as a spiritual teacher but do not believe in the incarnation of God in Jesus. Their Christology (such as it is) closely parallels ancient Gnosticism.

Rosicrucianism claims to embody and teach ancient wisdom that predates Christ and Christianity—an alternative wisdom tradition in the West with origins in ancient Egypt. Christianity is blended in via Gnosticism but Rosicrucianism claims to be older than Christianity. It is the higher wisdom, spiritual truth, allegedly known to all "adepts" (spiritually enlightened people) since the beginning of time. Jesus was such an adept but there have been many others. Rosicrucians who claim to be Christians consider Jesus the highest and best adept of ancient wisdom.

Rosicrucianism of this sort exists outside the boundaries of the label or any organization that so identifies itself. Another branch of the alternative reality/ancient wisdom tradition in the West (neo-Gnosticism) is Theosophy, which, like Rosicrucianism, transcends organizations that use that name. However, Theosophy blends Eastern mysticism with Western esotericism and often seems more Buddhist than Christian in flavor. One Theosophist who became disillusioned with its lack of emphasis on the uniqueness of Christ as savior was Swiss mystic, philosopher, and educator Rudolf Steiner (d. 1925) who founded a neo-Gnostic movement called *Anthroposophy* ("man-wisdom"). Anthroposophy is intellectual Rosicrucianism and mostly exoteric. It has strong Gnostic features although its members claim it to be Christian. The movement includes a denomination called The Christian Community. The best-known offshoot of Anthroposophy is the Waldorf School movement, which originally based its pedagogy on Steiner's "Spiritual Science."

Together, Rosicrucianism and Theosophy (including Anthroposophy) have spawned numerous neo-Gnostic sects and movements. Many of their teachings filtered into the so-called "New Age Movement" during the 1980s and filtered from there into mainstream European and American society—often blended with Eastern mysticism and paranormal experiences. Echoes of ancient Gnosticism can be heard in many New Age inspired teachings about the "Christ spirit" in each person as his or her "higher Self." Jesus was simply the human model of a "Christed" person—a person who lives fully in his or her higher spiritual Self detached from the world.

Echoes of Gnosticism in Popular Folk Religion

Esoteric Christianity is the purest form of Gnosticism in the modern world, but even it is neo-Gnostic, not pure ancient Gnosticism. A belief system that includes reincarnation can hardly be equated with ancient Gnosticism! The ancient Gnostics, whatever New Agers may say, did not believe in reincarnation. However, one does not have to stray far from the local church or Christian bookstore to find echoes of Gnosticism. Many gospel hymns and songs contain lyrics that sound decidedly Gnostic such as "like a bird from prison bars has flown, I'll fly away"[3]—referring to the death of a Christian. The "prison," of course, is the body. The "bird" is the immortal soul or spirit. Once one's ears are attuned to Gnosticism, its shadow appears all over the place. As suggested before, a person with ears and eyes attuned to Gnosticism begins to see it too often! An old saying has it that if one's only tool is a hammer everything becomes a nail. So it is with some students who become acquainted with Gnosticism; suddenly it's ubiquitous. So careful discernment is called for and part of that is keeping an eye on ancient Gnosticism as the criterion.

Folk religion is the informal, popular beliefs of people untutored in doctrine or theology. It thrives on comforting clichés and inspiring anecdotes that are often simply untrue. "Charity begins at home" and "God helps those who help themselves" are not in the Bible, but you would never know that by how often Christians preface them with "As the good book says!" Popular folk religion is riddled with echoes of Gnosticism.

One reason is that a shallow reading of the Bible can lead one to think it teaches that the body is sinful whereas the spirit is good. Paul, for example, often uses "flesh" for "fallen human nature," but few notice how the "works of the flesh" include spiritual sins that have nothing to do with the body. For Paul, "flesh" often simply meant "fallen human nature" and *not* the physical body. This confuses people who aren't taught how to read and understand the Bible. They equate "flesh" with "body" and conclude, like the ancient Gnostics, that the body is the seat of all sin. It's natural, then, to think of salvation as escape from the body and material existence.

Another reason for echoes of Gnosticism in folk religion is the natural tendency of sinful people (which we all are) to think of their "true selves" as divine. Again, a misreading of the Bible supports this false idea. Many Bible readers fail to distinguish between the human spirit and the Spirit of God.

They conflate the two as if the human spirit within is a spark of the divine Spirit—a decidedly Gnostic idea. A careful reading of the Bible reveals a clear difference between created spirit, which we all have, and God's own Holy Spirit, which, if we have him, is a gift, not a part of our natural equipment.

Finally, echoes of Gnosticism appear in folk religion because of the misunderstanding that religion, Christianity especially, promises escape from life's problems into a spiritual state of bliss through detachment from the world. As the old saying goes, some people are so heavenly minded they're no earthly good. They would say that's a good thing. Quietism is a form of Christian mysticism with Gnostic features. It emphasizes total detachment from the world in concentration on God through contemplation and prayer. The gospel, on the other hand, calls us to care for the world and to be good stewards of it through involvement in social ministry and evangelism. A popular Christian hymn says that if we turn our eyes upon Jesus "the things of earth will grow strangely dim."[4] That message echoes Gnostic disdain for physicality, for time, and for this world, which is only a place to escape, not a place to redeem by God's grace.

Antidotes to Gnosticism

Today, in the early twenty-first century, Gnosticism is not as direct a threat to New Testament, apostolic, orthodox Christianity as it was in the second century. Nevertheless, Gnostic-like beliefs pop up among Christians—both filtering in from neo-Gnostic groups and those influenced by them and appearing as popular folk religion. Christians should look first to themselves and ask what elements of Gnosticism infect their beliefs about creation, God, Jesus Christ, salvation, and life after death. For example, many Christians know little or nothing about traditional Christian belief about the future resurrection of all the dead. They believe in the immortality of souls or spirits and find comfort in the idea that those who died in faith are already enjoying the fullness of heaven—in a disembodied, purely spiritual state. That is closer to Gnosticism than to orthodox Christianity. The Apostle Paul refuted such in 1 Corinthians 15—an entire chapter devoted to affirming that bodily resurrection, Christ's and ours, is part and parcel of the gospel of Jesus Christ. That is our "blessed hope."

Also, Christian pastors and teachers need to be alert to inroads of neo-Gnostic ideas seeping into their churches and influencing their people from sources such as the so-called New Age Movement. Underlying that is belief that all reality is some form or manifestation of God and that the human soul or spirit is a "spark of the divine." It's not uncommon to hear Christians talking that way about their souls. What is at stake is the transcendence of God, God's otherness. Also at stake is original sin itself—the first and most basic sin being idolatry of self. Pastors and Christian teachers should find opportunities to refute such popular ideas as antithetical to the gospel and dangerous to spiritual well-being.

One helpful antidote to Gnosticism among Christians is sound Bible study. Bible teachers (pastors, Sunday school teachers, writers of Sunday school curricula) should explain Paul's frequent use of "flesh" (KJV, NIV, NRSV) as shorthand for "fallen human nature" or rather for "selfish desires" (CEB) and not for the body—especially when he is talking about sin. This causes great confusion among theologically untrained Bible readers; it's natural that they assume "flesh" connected with "sin" means that the body is the seat of sin and evil. That is not Paul's intention. When flesh (selfish desires) and sin are associated in Paul's writing in the New Testament the connection is not between body and sin but between selfish desires and sin.

Great emphasis on the incarnation as absolutely crucial to the gospel is perhaps the best antidote to Gnostic tendencies that creep into Christians' thinking. Christians need gently to correct fellow Christians who say that Jesus was God with human skin—as if his humanity were only skin deep and he was not human "all the way down." Studying various Bible translations can help; for example the Common English Bible (CEB) uses "Human One" as a corrective to reading "Son of Man" to mean "Son of God." Docetism is rampant especially among conservative Christians who think they are paying Jesus compliments by thinking of him as other than truly human. They need to be reminded that true humanity is not fallen humanity and fallen humanity is "damaged goods." Jesus was the true human; we are poor copies because of sin. What Jesus came to do was to restore our true humanity in God's image and likeness, not liberate us from humanity.

Bringing It Home

1. Gnosticism was not just a set of doctrines; it was an attitude about time, matter, and who humans are in relation to God. Why might some people aspire to the "special knowledge"?

2. What does it say about Jesus that he was human *and* divine?

3. How do our church ministries care for people's physical needs? How we do care for people's spiritual needs? Is one more important than the other? What might it mean that God cares for your body as well as your soul?

4. Do you know Christians who believe in reincarnation? Do you know Christians who believe that the human soul is a divine spark?

5. How might Bible study and small group study help correct some of these deeply held, nonbiblical beliefs?

6. Discuss your thoughts about groups such as Rosicrucians and Theosophists. Why do Eastern religions appeal to so many American Christians?

Chapter 4

Messing with Divine Revelation

Montanism and Marcionism

What Is "God's Word?"

Throughout the Christian centuries most Christians have equated "God's Word" with "revelation" with "Holy Scripture." Unknown to most modern Christians, however, is how complicated the process of identifying scripture was in the early church. No universal consensus existed about what "books" constituted the Christian Bible until the late fourth century and that probably would not have happened without some pressure from Roman emperors. An influential fourth-century Egyptian Christian bishop named Athanasius circulated a letter at Easter in 367 in which he listed all twenty-seven books of the New Testament. That "canon" of Christian writings was not new, but before 367 it was disputed. After 367, it was almost universally accepted throughout Christendom. Christians also accepted the thirty-nine books of the Hebrew canon (twenty-two in Jewish Bibles) as inspired. Some Christians came to accept more Old Testament books as inspired; these came to be known as the Apocrypha but were later thrown out of the Bible by Protestant reformers such as Luther.

The "canonization process" was long, complicated, and arduous with many twists and turns. Different churches throughout the Roman Empire accepted different books as inspired scripture—God's written Word to humanity. Three criteria played into such decisions and different churches put different weight on them. First, whether a book was written by an apostle or by someone very close to an apostle was crucial, but some writings were disputed and some that had no direct connection with any apostle were highly revered (e.g., the "Shepherd of Hermas" by the Roman Christians). Second, Christians wanted to know if a book was old, going back to the first century, and whether it was nearly universally accepted. Third, Christians judged disputed books by their content. Did they communicate inspiring messages from God necessary for salvation and Christian living?

Ultimately, some books got into the New Testament in 367 that were not widely considered inspiring and were widely disputed just because, finally, they were judged to be written by an apostle or someone very close to an apostle. An example is 3 John; another is Jude. Jude was believed to be Jesus's brother, so that little "book" was finally included. By 367, most Christians, especially bishops, argued that the Holy Spirit guided the process to this final conclusion and that it was time to close the Christian canon. Without such there was less authority for fighting heresies.

Someone should not misunderstand by thinking that up until 367 there was no agreement about the Christian writings that were inspired and constituted God's written word—like the prophets of the Hebrew Bible. There was wide and deep agreement, but a few books (like Hebrews) were still being disputed by some Christians because there was no certainty about their authorship and some churches didn't possess them. But Athanasius did not "create the canon." He simply closed it and brought the process and dispute to an end. (Of course the dispute about the Apocrypha rose in the Reformation, but that's a different matter.)

Again, heresy was the mother of orthodoxy. Certain second-century (and later) heresies forced the church to consider the question of a closed canon of Christian scriptures. Without them, it may never have happened, at least not in the same way or as soon.

There can be no doubt that the closing of the Christian canon, or at least the New Testament, was a momentous event in the life of Christianity. One could compare it with the writing and affirming of the United States Constitution in 1789. Between 1776 and 1789, the United States had no unifying constitution; the final acceptance of it by all the states became an irreversible decision that changed the character of the nation. But nobody questions it just because it resulted from a process that included much controversy.

The Bible did not fall out of the sky from heaven. I once saw a book written by a fundamentalist pastor entitled *That Manuscript from Heaven*. The title, if not the contents, implied that the Bible simply fell out of heaven to earth whole. That's not what happened. A basic Christian faith affirmation is that the Holy Spirit of God inspired these writings and led the early Christian churches to recognize them as inspired and authoritative for faith and practice.

But what heresies propelled the early Christians to identify and close the canon of scripture? And where are those heresies today? Do they still exist among Christians? Or are there at least distant echoes of them still reverberating among Christians? That's what this chapter will explain.

Montanism Challenges the Canon

The word *canon*, in this sense, means "rule" or "measure." It's like a measuring stick. It also means a collection of recognized writings. Modern scholars debate the appropriate canon of literature students should study in college courses. There was no formal, official, closed canon of Christian scriptures in the second century—except the Hebrew scriptures (which canon was closed by Jewish rabbis in the late first century). Various writings (henceforth "books") circulated among Christians and carried varying degrees of authority depending on how they were received by churches. One circulating in the Middle East as early as the turn of the first century into the second was the Didache or "The Teaching." Many churches in Syria, for example, considered it scripture. Eventually, however, it was not included in the official canon because nobody knew who wrote it and it had no apparent connection with an apostle. By that time, around 100, most of the books that later were included in the canon (in 367) were known and circulated and quoted by bishops— leaders of Christian churches in cities around the empire. But some were known only in one area while others were known only in other areas. There were other books such as the "Shepherd of Hermas" that Christians in and around Rome revered but that Christians in Egypt, for example, knew nothing about until much later. Again, it was excluded from the canon because nobody knew who wrote it. But Hebrews was included because of a popular and widespread belief that it was written by an apostle although there was no proof which apostle wrote it.

By the middle of the second century, the idea of a closed canon of authoritative Christian books was "in the air," so to speak, and several churches in the empire were treating their own favorite collections as that. But especially Middle Eastern (Syrian) Christianity was charismatic, believing prophecy, for example, was still a gift given to special people and that prophetic utterances by known and highly regarded prophets should be believed. Such Christians did not want to "chase the Holy Spirit into a book." Wandering Christian prophets visited such churches where they were treated almost as if they carried the authority of an apostle, but the Didache set down rules for how they should be evaluated and treated. It's not as if anything they said or did was automatically accepted. One can easily see how this became a problem. How do you judge utterances of a prophet without a closed canon of inspired books believed to be authored by God himself? And so many Christians began to turn away from prophets and their prophetic messages and invest themselves more in books believed to be apostolic.

Into this milieu of some confusion over "God's word" stepped a man named Montanus. He was a convert to Christianity and lived in a city of Asia Minor (modern Turkey) known as Pepuza. But he traveled around the Roman Empire establishing his own churches based on his inspired prophecies. These churches were called "The New Prophecy"—perhaps the first schism within Christianity. The bishops appointed by apostles and the ones they appointed rejected Montanus and his New Prophecy churches. Montanus was considered a self-appointed upstart, if not a charlatan. Much controversy exists among scholars about Montanus. We do not know enough about him. What we do know, from contemporary sources, is that he claimed the Holy Spirit took control of his vocal chords and "played" on them like one plays on a harp. In other words, he claimed that when he uttered prophecies he was speaking God's own word and Christians ought to listen, believe, and obey. He rejected the exclusive claims of bishops to "apostolic succession" and authority, and he rejected any identification of God's word with a book or books.

During the lifetime and ministry of Montanus (approximately the middle of the second century) there was no official Christian canon. But there was an unofficial and widely recognized canon even if its precise contents were disputed and varied from church to church. But most Christians treated certain Christian writings as especially authoritative—at least in the sense of ruling out doctrines and teachings they clearly contradicted. Montanus did not reject all inspired writings, but he did believe God's word continues to be given through prophets such as himself. His enemies, mostly bishops, claimed that he was a fanatic and a grave danger to the order of Christianity. They claimed that he called his followers to leave their churches and come to Pepuza to wait with him for the imminent return of Christ—which he revealed would happen there. His followers were allegedly encouraged to be celibate even if married. Eventually two women prophets attached to him and prophesied with him.

If this phenomenon of Montanism or New Prophecy had been limited to one or two rural churches in Syria, nobody would have paid any attention. The problem was that it struck a chord with many Christians who worried that Christianity in the Roman Empire was becoming dead, formal, ritualistic, and hierarchical. "Where was the Spirit?" they asked. The problem was not that Montanus was a prophet; the problem was that he claimed his prophecies were above critique or correction and were just as authoritative as the writings of the apostles (or at least that's what contemporary sources say about him).

One problem is that we really do not know that much about Montanus himself. We know more about later Montanism, the New Prophecy movement that lasted for a century or more and spread throughout the Roman Empire. Whether Montanus should be blamed for all its excesses is debated. But "Montanism" is bigger than Montanus and rightly or wrongly he is its historical symbol. Montanism has come to be a synonym for any emphasis on inspired, authoritative prophecy that goes beyond scripture and claims to communicate "new truths" to be believed by all Christians.

Montanism probably contributed greatly to the demise of charismatic gifts among Christians—at least in the catholic and orthodox churches of the Roman Empire and afterward. It also propelled forward the felt need for a closed canon of authoritative Christian scriptures.

Marcionism also Challenges the Canon

Marcion was a Christian leader in Rome at the same time Montanus was prophesying in Asia Minor. Many things about Marcion's life and teachings are uncertain, but he was probably a Christian bishop who moved to Rome to have greater influence. There, around 140, he proposed two ideas that leaders of Roman Christian congregations deemed heretical. Much of what we think we know about Marcion comes from antiheretical writings by later church fathers, especially Origen who wrote a treatise "Against Marcion." But most scholars think Origen was fair in his descriptions of those he and other orthodox Christians considered heretics.

Marcion was not exactly a Gnostic, but some of his teachings overlapped with theirs and for that reason he is sometimes lumped together with them. The main Marcionite teaching that resonated with Gnosticism was that the God that Christians worship, the Father of Jesus Christ, did not create the world. Rather, according to Marcion, the world was created by a demented god, whom he identified with Yahweh, the God worshipped by Jews. Marcion was virulently anti-Jewish, not because he was anti-Semitic in the modern sense, but because he was angry with Jews for their treatment of Christians. Sometime in the late first century, leading rabbis had sent word throughout the Roman Empire to expel Christians from synagogues. Jews were given special exemptions from certain Roman laws; Marcion was bitter because those exemptions did not apply to Christians once Jews expelled them from synagogues. Well, at least that's one theory about his anti-Jewish attitudes.

Marcion is best remembered in the annals of church history, however, for being the first Christian to propose a canon of Christian scriptures that would entirely exclude the Hebrew scriptures *and* any Christian writings that were "too Jewish." The Marcion canon was a very truncated canon that included only Gentile writings—Luke and Acts (Luke was not a Jew) and edited versions of Paul's epistles. Marcion wanted to expunge even from Paul's letters anything he considered too Jewish.

Over the centuries, the term *Marcionism* has come to be used by orthodox Christians for any Christian attempt to exclude the Old Testament from the Christian Bible. Usually this does not take the form of an explicit campaign to exclude it; usually it appears as an ignoring of the Old Testament with the excuse that "it's irrelevant to Christians." German theologian Friedrich Schleiermacher, the "father of modern liberal theology," said of the Old Testament that it "lacked the normative dignity of the New."[1] Many German theologians agreed and left the Old Testament alone. (On the other hand, some of the greatest Old Testament scholars, both Jewish and Christian, have been German!)

Marcion has gone down in the memory of orthodox Christianity of all denominations as an early "arch-heretic," one who almost derailed Christianity at its beginnings. He had many followers and some churches in Rome and elsewhere followed him and adopted his truncated canon. The leading bishops and theologians, however, excommunicated Marcion and his followers. (This was at a time, of course, when "excommunication" had no "teeth" so Marcion and his followers continued to consider themselves the "true Christians" and, like Montanus's New Prophecy, formed a schism to rival the catholic and orthodox churches.)

Roman Christians Respond to Marcion

About 170, Christian leaders in Rome developed what has come to be known as the "Muratorian Canon"—a list of authoritative Christian writings—the first official listing of books of a New Testament (although it doesn't state them as such). The canon was clearly made to counter Marcion's truncated, anti-Jewish canon. The text surrounding the list mentions Marcion as a heretic. Nobody knows exactly who created the list and it never became the official one for all Christians everywhere. Athanasius's 367 CE list did not correspond with it completely. Most scholars think the Muratorian Canon was simply the New Testament in embryo—an attempt to get the ball rolling, so to speak, to lead Christians away from Marcionism toward a fuller Christian Bible. But it probably does reflect books many, perhaps most, Christians in Rome (other than Marcion and his followers) considered inspired and authoritative.

The Muratorian Canon listed the following as true and authoritative Christian scriptures: the four Gospels (Matthew, Mark, Luke, and John), Acts of the Apostles, the thirteen letters of Paul that are in the New Testament now, 1 and 2 John, Jude, Revelation, and "Wisdom of Solomon," "Revelation of Peter" (although called "questionable"), and the "Shepherd of Hermas." However the text surrounding the list (in what is known as the "Muratorian Fragment") says the last one should not be read in church, meaning it is for private devotion only. Eventually, of course, Hebrews, 1 and 2 Peter, and 3 John were added to the New Testament (they were already considered scripture by other Christians outside Rome) and the last three listed above were dropped (Christians outside Rome did not know of them or did not consider them scripture).

Why Montanism and Marcionism Are Heresies

Off and on throughout church history, but especially in modern times, sympathies for Montanism and Marcionism have arisen among groups of Christians. Should people in second-century Christianity, before there was even a standard set of orthodox doctrines fully developed, be considered heretics? Let's be clear about something. Nobody claims that Montanus or his followers were evil people out to destroy Christianity. Misguided, perhaps and probably. But not evil or even sinister. The word *heretic* often evokes such thoughts, but it shouldn't. Heretics can be well intentioned and even profoundly spiritual. The problem has nothing to do with their personalities or spiritualities; it has to do with the effects of their teachings on other Christians and especially on the churches.

So let's begin with Montanus. He has many modern defenders—especially among Pentecostals and charismatics. By most accounts he was sincere and deeply spiritual. He was afraid that Christianity was abandoning its early passion and losing the living presence and activity of the Holy Spirit. No doubt the catholic bishops overreacted, suppressing prophecy and the other "supernatural" gifts of the Holy Spirit. One can regret (as I do) that the church generally turned from defining the true church from where the Spirit is to where the bishop is. It was an overreaction to Montanism and the New Prophecy.

Still, Montanism, whether Montanus was himself guilty of it, is wrong. Why? Because it opens the door to total confusion. Without inspired and authoritative scripture and without Christian leaders steeped in both scripture and tradition, how are prophecies to be judged? Many people see Mormonism as one example of modern Montanism. The president of the Church of Jesus Christ of Latter-day Saints (Mormon) is its chief prophet who can pronounce new truths and it remains open to new revelations that add to scripture. Anyone familiar with Pentecostalism and the charismatic movement can easily see the dangers of Montanism around their fringes. (By far the majority of Pentecostal and charismatic leaders recognize this and judge all prophecies by scripture, but there are numerous independent prophets who claim their teachings add to scripture if not supersede it.)

Similarly, Marcion may have been a deeply spiritual Christian man. His character may have been above reproach. But his virulent anti-Jewish form of

Christianity was dangerous and distorted the record of Christian history itself by forgetting that Jesus was a Jew—not only ethnically but religiously. And his limiting of inspired Christian scriptures to Gentile writings attempted totally to disconnect Christianity from its Hebrew background and divorce Yahweh from God the Father of Jesus Christ. Later Marcionism does not necessarily echo Marcion's anti-Jewish sentiments, but it cuts up the Bible, holding some parts in higher esteem than others. Scripture is then mutilated and Christians miss much that the Bible has to say that challenges them. When we ignore portions of the Bible, or demote them to less-than-inspired status, we often do that because of our vested interests. We want scripture to reflect our preferred beliefs and lifestyles, so we focus on portions that we think do that and overlook or ignore ones that don't.

Modern Montanism

Montanism, or beliefs and practices like it, has appeared repeatedly in Christian history. During the Reformation, a group of radical reformers challenged Luther and the other mainline reformers, because they wanted the churches to be led by the Spirit and not by a book. This diverse group of radical reformers has been known by scholars as "the spirituals" or "the spiritualists" of the Reformation. They were the charismatics of the sixteenth century (although not all charismatic Christians place prophecies over the Bible). Luther despised these people, calling them *Die Schwärmer*, which means the "rabble" or even "vermin." He and the other mainline Reformers were trying to reemphasize the Bible as the supreme source and norm for all Christian belief and practice (*Sola Scriptura*); he worried that the "spirituals" among Protestants would undermine the whole effort to reform the church and open the door to chaos and spiritual anarchy. When they came to him proclaiming "The Spirit! The Spirit!" tradition has it that Luther replied, "I smite thy 'Spirit' on the snout." And Luther is supposed to have commented that they "swallowed the Spirit feathers and all." (Luther was given to strong language about people with whom he disagreed.)

During the eighteenth century, a Swedish prophet named Emanuel Swedenborg published new revelations allegedly given to him in dreams and visions; his followers considered these equal with scripture and necessary for understanding scripture correctly. Swedenborg had many followers.

Famous nineteenth-century American agriculturalist Johnny Appleseed (John Chapman) was actually a Swedenborgian missionary. Wherever he went planting apple orchards he left Swedenborg's writings. Helen Keller, the blind and deaf American writer, was a Swedenborgian. Throughout America one can find Swedenborgian churches called "Church of the New Jerusalem."

When Joseph Smith began publishing his writings such as *The Book of Mormon* and *The Pearl of Great Price* and added these to scripture as equally inspired and authoritative, many critics equated him and his followers (Latter-day Saints) with the ancient New Prophecy movement of Montanus. Early Mormons even spoke in tongues and prophesied.

The Pentecostal movement was born in 1906 at the Azusa Street Revival in Los Angeles (although there had been pre-Pentecostal phenomena beginning for more than a decade before). Pentecostals (who a century later number in the many millions) are diverse; some elevate scripture above prophecies (including "interpretations of tongues"), but some value modern prophecies as highly as scripture. During the 1980s, a group known as the Kansas City Prophets began to reemphasize prophecy in a way that even other Pentecostals criticized. One leader claimed (though not all agreed) that he was the Apostle Paul's "successor" and that Paul would be astonished if he knew the new revelations being given by God through him and other prophets.

Another branch of Pentecostalism arose in Tulsa, Oklahoma in the 1970s and flourished throughout America and the world in the 1990s and beyond. Some call it the "Word Faith" movement because its leaders emphasize prosperity and health through positive speaking ("words of faith"). The movement was founded by a Pentecostal evangelist who claimed to be receiving *rhema* from God. According to him and his followers, *rhema* (a Greek word for "word") is God's word for today that was not revealed in scripture. Word Faith evangelists and teachers (again, not all charismatics fall into that category) distinguish "logos" from "rhema" with the former designating past revelation—mainly in scripture—and the latter designating contemporary revelation through prophets. The distinction is not supported by Greek scholars.

As with Gnosticism, it is tempting to use *Montanism* to cover too much; not every person or group who believes in contemporary prophets or prophecy is Montanist. The term should be reserved for those who wish to elevate contemporary prophecies (whether called that or not) to equal authority with scripture or authority greater than scripture.

Modern Marcionism

The term *Marcionism* is used by scholars *only* for individuals or groups that want to expel the Hebrew scriptures from the Christian Bible *or* who treat the Old Testament as worthless except as literature. Friedrich Schleiermacher, mentioned in an earlier chapter, is an example. Many liberal theologians after him, especially Germans, followed his idea of the Old Testament as "lacking the normative dignity of the New Testament." What he and they meant was that the Old Testament does not adequately communicate "God conscious-ness" to us and even falls short of supporting Christian character, conduct, and belief. Schleiermacher did not cast the Old Testament out of Christian Bibles (as Luther did the Apocrypha), but he treated it much like Luther treated the New Testament Epistle of James—as "full of straw" (not spiritu-ally nourishing). Nobody in modern times thinks, as Marcion did, that a de-mented or evil God inspired the Hebrew scriptures, so modern Marcionism is not an exact replica of what Marcion taught. But it always denigrates the Old Testament in some way even if only by ignoring it.

During the Nazi era in Germany many German theologians and bibli-cal scholars dismissed the Old Testament because of its "Jewishness." This was blatant, obvious Marcionism politically motivated and driven by anti-Semitism. After World War II such theologians and biblical scholars were condemned and often expelled from professional societies. Their reputations were ruined by their anti-Semitism even as others sometimes dismissed the Old Testament, not for its "Jewishness" but for its allegedly primitive views of God.

Admitting that the Old Testament contains stories that do not espe-cially glorify God, and claiming that Jesus Christ and faith in him relativizes much that one reads in the Old Testament is *not* Marcionism. Marcionism appears when someone goes further and denies the inspiration and authority of the whole Old Testament and restricts "revelation for today" to the New Testament or even portions of it.

During the middle of the twentieth century, several Christian groups arose that took dispensationalism to an extreme. *Dispensationalism* is an interpre-tation of the Bible that regards it as containing different "programs" for sal-vation. God's way of salvation for Jews, for example, was different than for Gentiles. Most dispensationalists believe that the Gentile church is not God's "new Israel" but a kind of divine "plan B" because Israel rejected Jesus as its messiah. According to dispensationalism, after the "rapture" of Christians, God will return to dealing especially with Israel who are God's chosen people forever.

Some dispensationalists began to theorize that even the New Testament contains portions relevant to Jews and portions relevant to Gentile Christians. Repeating one of Marcion's errors, they relegate "Jewish" parts of the New Testament such as Matthew (written to Jews) and Hebrews (also written to Jews) to secondary status and do not see them as especially relevant to Gentile Christians. They place emphasis on Luke, Acts, and Paul's epistles instead—again, a truncated biblical canon. All sixty-six books of the Bible are in their Bibles, but they *interpret* parts as more authoritative than others.

Perhaps it is right, or at least not totally wrong, to talk about a "popular Marcionism" that is rampant among Christians in the twenty-first century. That is the tendency of many Christians to ignore the Old Testament or to select a "canon within the canon" and ignore other parts of the Bible. Again, most often this is due to an unconscious desire for the Bible to support already chosen and favored beliefs. For example, some Christians act as if the Acts of the Apostles isn't even in the Bible because they are so afraid of supernatural, ecstatic experiences promoted by Pentecostals and charismatics. Others act as if the Revelation of John is not in the Bible because it's so difficult to understand and so many people get obsessed with "end times" speculation. Others act as if the Epistle of James isn't in the Bible because Luther didn't like it and it seems (to them) to promote salvation by works.

Antidotes to Montanism and Marcionism

One way to avoid Montanism in any form is to evaluate all messages, whether "prophetic" or not, by scripture, tradition, reason, and experience and to reject messages that claim to be from God but that contradict scripture or add "new truths" to scripture. Does God still speak today? Saying yes does not make a person a Montanist. Saying no does seem to chase the Holy Spirit into a book. But prophecies and other contemporary messages from God cannot be given the same weight as scripture or be used to control or abuse people or to elevate the prophet to special spiritual status.

I have developed five criteria for evaluating contemporary messages claiming to be from God.[2] First, the "Christ Touchstone." If a prophecy promotes Christ and not the prophet it *may* be valid. Second, the "Apostolic

Norm." If the message is consistent with the gospel found in the apostles' writings in the New Testament it *may* be valid. Third, the "Unity Criterion." If a prophecy does not promote spiritual elitism or schism, it *may* be valid. Fourth, the "Sanity Check." If a message does not require the sacrifice of the intellect and mindless acceptance of newly revealed teachings, it *may* be valid. Fifth, the "Messiah Test." If the prophecy does not exalt some individual into an object of veneration, it *may* be valid.

Notice that no criterion absolutely validates a prophecy or new Christian message. There is no litmus test to replace discernment, and discernment has to be based on knowledge of the Bible, inward guidance of the Holy Spirit, the careful evaluation of a group of thoughtful people of God, and just plain reason (logic).

The best antidote to Marcionism is reverence (not worship) for scripture, reading and study of *all* of scripture, and preaching and teaching *through* scripture. This is one reason many Christian churches follow a uniform "lectionary" for Sunday scripture readings and texts for sermons—to avoid congregations and pastors from becoming locked into a particular portion of the Bible to the neglect of the rest. The lectionary usually goes through all of scripture in a cycle of several years and then begins over again. Humble submission to *all* of God's word in scripture underlies this antidote and is necessary to avoid unconscious Marcionism.

Every thinking Christian recognizes the problems in the Old Testament (and perhaps some in the New Testament as well). Holy wars and ethnic cleansing supposedly commanded by God stand out as particularly troubling to many people. One does not have to interpret all of the Old Testament literally or even consider it infallible in order to hear God speaking through it. Christological interpretation of the whole of scripture, including the Old Testament, is not Marcionism. If more Christians practiced interpreting the whole Bible through Jesus Christ, as witness to him and judged by him, Marcionism would not be such a temptation. Jesus Christ is God's Word in person; scripture, all of it, is the unique, inspired witness to him.

Bringing It Home

1. In your opinion why is having an agreed-upon canon of scripture important for your church? Why is it important to have Christian leaders steeped in both scripture and tradition?

2. What are your favorite books of the Bible? Why? Are there parts of the Bible that trouble you? If so, give an example. Why would the early church only accept books that were written by an apostle or eyewitness?

3. Do you believe, generally speaking, that the Old Testament is as important or authoritative as the New Testament? How is the Old Testament important for Christian faith and practice? Are there parts of the Bible that you would like to ignore?

4. When persons say that God spoke to them, how do you evaluate what is said? No Christian wants the faith to be dead, so what is the role of the Holy Spirit in keeping faith vital?

5. Who are people who proclaim that they are prophets today? Are there people who believe that some modern prophecy goes beyond scripture and claims to be new truth from God?

6. How do you understand salvation? Are there different programs for different groups, like Jews and/or Gentiles? Is saying that there are many paths to God the same as saying that God has different ways of saving different people?

7. Reread the author's five criteria for evaluating contemporary messages that claim to be from God. How can they be helpful?

Chapter 5

Doubting the Deity of Jesus Christ

Adoptionism, Arianism, and Nestorianism

The Foundational Christian Truth: Jesus Is God

During the 1990s and first decade of the twenty-first century, several popular books and movies based on these books claimed that the deity of Jesus Christ and the Trinity were inventions of Christian bishops under Roman Emperor Constantine, the first "Christian" Roman emperor, in the fourth century. Allegedly, earlier Christians thought of Jesus as just a man, even if a very special one.

Anyone who has studied second-century Christian writings and anti-Christian writings knows better. The anti-Christian Roman orator Celsus criticized second-century Christians for worshipping "a man as God." Second-century Christian writers such as Justin Martyr proclaimed Jesus as God incarnate. The first great Christian theologians were Irenaeus, Origen, and Tertullian—all living and writing around 200 CE. One finds in their writings clear evidence of belief in Jesus as God as well as human.

The truth is that Christian bishops and theologians of the fourth century, during the reign of Constantine and afterward, found it necessary to defend the full deity and humanity of Christ in a way not required before. Before Constantine, Christian bishops could not unite as they could under his rule. In 325, Constantine called all Christian bishops to meet to discuss a controversy about the deity of Christ. The result was the Nicene Creed, which only reaffirmed what Christians had believed for centuries—that Jesus was and is "truly God and truly human"—of the "same substance" with the Father. A later, fuller version of the creed (381) would add the Holy Spirit because some Christians were questioning the distinct personhood of the Spirit as one substance with the Father and the Son.

The fourth-century developments added nothing new to what Christians had always believed—except language to make it more clear and precise so as to avoid heresies that denied the deity of Christ and the Trinity.

The incarnation of God in Christ is a doctrine firmly rooted in the New Testament itself. John 1 expresses it clearly: "In the beginning was the Word and the Word [*logos*] was with God and was God. . . . The Word became flesh and made his home among us" (vv. 1, 14). But was the "Word" God or "a god?" Some Christians raised that question in the first part of the fourth century because they wanted to emphasize the oneness of God (monotheism). Christian bishops and theologians had to explain again, and express without any ambiguity, that Jesus Christ was and is the incarnation (becoming human) of God the Son, the eternal Word of God, equal with the Father.

This is not the place for a full explanation or defense of the deity of Jesus Christ; that has been done numerous times before. Suffice it to say that Jesus said he was "one with the Father" and that if people saw him they saw the Father. First John says that anyone who does not have the Son does not have the Father. Jesus forgave sins—not in God's name but by his own authority, as if he were God who had been sinned against. C. S. Lewis has a great chapter on this issue of the deity of Christ in *Mere Christianity* where he lays out the famous "liar, lunatic, or Son of God" argument. Jesus made claims about himself that, if true, amounted to claiming to be God. (He was formally accused of making himself equal with God at his trial.) If his claims were not true, he was either a liar or a lunatic. Few people want to say that about Jesus!

The incarnation is the heart, the center, and the core of Christian belief. It is what sets Christianity apart from all other religions and is inseparable from other basic Christian beliefs. The early Christians proclaimed loudly and often that if Jesus was not God *and* human, he could not save us. Only a human being could suffer the penalty for sins; only God could offer himself as a perfect sacrifice. Only a person who was *both* God and human could be the mediator reconciling God and humanity. This is why the World Council of Churches requires member denominations to affirm that "Jesus Christ is God and Savior." Anything less is a pale imitation of Christianity. What is at stake with Jesus's deity is the gospel itself.

However, throughout Christian history some Christians have doubted or denied the deity of Jesus Christ. Time and again the churches have faced this problem. The first universal council of bishops in 325 was not the first meeting of Christian leaders to address denials of Jesus's deity by Christians. We will begin our story of heresies about the deity of Christ with a man who denied it and a group of bishops who met to excommunicate him and denounce his teaching as heresy.

Adoptionism Denies the Deity of Christ in Third-Century Syria

One of the first major rows about the deity of Jesus Christ in Christianity began with the teaching of a Christian leader in Syria in the middle of the third century. His name was Paul and he was from Samosata, a city in Syria. He became bishop of the Christians in Antioch, a major center of early Christianity, in 260. As bishop of Antioch he had great influence on Christians throughout the eastern half of the Roman Empire. Antioch is where Christians were first called "Christians" and a center of the Apostle Paul's missionary activity. It is where Peter and Paul had their confrontation about Gentiles becoming Christians without first becoming Jewish (by means of circumcision). By the third century, the city and surrounding area had numerous Christian churches. Paul was their leader.

Most of what we know about Paul of Samosata's teaching about Christ comes from his critics—other bishops and church fathers who strongly disagreed with him, such as the first Christian historian Eusebius about a century later. So some scholars have cast doubt on what Paul of Samosata really taught (as is often the case with early heretics). The issue here, for our purposes, is not Paul himself or what he actually taught (which we may not be sure about) but the nature of the heresy that in church history is traced back to him—*adoptionism*.

74

Apparently, if the sources are to be believed, Paul did not believe Jesus began life as God incarnate but rather began life as a mere human being with potential to become "divine"—God's special "son." At his baptism in the Jordan River by John the Baptist, so historical adoptionism says, God "adopted" Jesus into a unique and very special relationship with himself so that they became "Father" and "Son." But Jesus remained ontologically (as to his substance, his being) only human. The result of this adoption of Jesus by God into sonship was only that Jesus became the unique human instrument of God in revealing himself to people and saving them from their sins. But Jesus was never of the same substance as God.

Paul's adoptionist Christology is sometimes called "monarchianism" and specified as "dynamic monarchianism" to distinguish it from other forms of monarchianism. *Monarchianism* is a word used by early Christians and later theologians to describe *any* belief in the absolute oneness of God. All forms of it deny the real triunity of God, the Trinity. In Paul's case, only the Father is God; the son Jesus is a man taken by God into a special relationship with himself. Thus, it's called "dynamic monarchianism" because it implies that God can *become* Father (rather than be eternally Father). (The next chapter, about trinitarian heresies, will explain "modalistic monarchianism," which is quite different from the dynamic version.)

Paul of Samosata's reasons for denying the real, ontological deity of Christ probably had something to do with a strong desire to emphasize Christianity as a monotheistic religion to distinguish it from the polytheism of many pagans in the Roman Empire. He may also have been reaching out to Jews who were scandalized by the doctrine of incarnation and the deity of the man Jesus.

Adoptionism has come to be used as a term for any doctrine or teaching that reduces Jesus to a mere human being—however highly exalted in relation with God. Whether Jesus's special sonship with God began at his baptism or earlier or later is not crucial to adoptionism. What is crucial is the idea that Jesus "became" divine and God's unique Son and never was God incarnate, one in substance with God the Father.

A group of seventy Christian bishops from around the Middle East met at Antioch in 269 and deposed Paul as bishop of Antioch because of his teaching about Christ. This was the earliest large gathering of Christian bishops and was only possible because of a lull in persecutions of Christians by Roman emperors and governors.

Arianism Denies the Deity of Jesus Christ in Fourth-Century Egypt

The biggest row in the history of Christian doctrine, at least before the Reformation, began in Alexandria, Egypt in 318. Alexandria was the second richest and most powerful city of the Roman Empire, and it was the home of many Christians. It was also a center of intellectual life, including a Christian seminary. In 318, Constantine was sitting on the empire's throne and gradually moving it to a new city he was building called Constantinople. Constantine officially legalized Christianity and began to favor it in 313— soon after becoming emperor. He was disturbed to hear that Christians in Egypt were arguing over the deity of Christ. So he called a universal ("ecumenical") council of all Christian bishops to Nicea where he was temporarily living while the new capital was being built.

The background to the council and its decisions and the great controversy that ensued was an argument between Alexander, the bishop of Alexandria, and Arius, a leading priest of Alexandria who probably wanted to be bishop. Arius openly denied the full and true deity of Jesus Christ and led his followers through the streets of Alexandria chanting "There was a time when the Son was not."[1] Alexander tried to discipline Arius and put down his heresy, but Arius just became louder and more vehement in his denials of the deity of Christ.

Arius, unlike Paul of Samosata, did not deny that Jesus Christ was the incarnation of a preexisting "divine" being. According to Arius, Jesus was not a mere man "adopted" by God into special sonship. He was more than a great prophet. He was the Word, the Logos, the first and greatest creature God ever made become incarnate as a human being through the virgin Mary. But the Word, the Son of God, was created in time and not equal with the Father. He was god two (but not "God, too!")—a glorious creature worthy of worship but not of the same substance as God the Father.

Arius denied not only the deity of Christ but also the Trinity. According to him, God is not three persons sharing one divine substance, essence, or nature. God is one person—the Father—creating a replica of himself, a great spiritual being called the Logos or Word, but remaining solely eternal God with all the powers of God.

Alexander called all the bishops of Egypt together in 318 to settle this controversy. Fighting between Arius's followers and Alexander's had broken

76

out in churches and in the streets of the city. Pamphlets by both sides excoriated the other. Arius claimed Alexander and the trinitarian Christians were polytheists—believers in more than one God. Alexander and his followers claimed Arius was a new adoptionist in disguise. After all, even if Christ preexisted the birth of Jesus, he was still in some sense subordinate to the Father as in adoptionism and therefore not truly savior, lord, and worshipful God.

The bishops stripped Arius of his rank as a church leader (archdeacon) and they declared his doctrine, "subordinationism," as heresy. Schism threatened. Arius would not give up and his followers continued to oppose Alexander and the doctrine of the Trinity.

Constantine's called council in 325 was supposed to settle the matter. Over three hundred bishops came. Constantine presided over their deliberations and demanded that they decide once and for all what Christians are to believe about Jesus Christ in relation to God. The council began with a reading of Arius's teaching by a bishop who supported him. (Arius could not be in the council because he was not a bishop.) When he got to the part about Jesus not being God, another bishop grabbed the parchment, threw it on the floor, and stomped on it. A near riot broke out. Constantine had to call in guards to calm down the bishops and their assistants.

Eventually calm prevailed and a creed was written. The Nicene Creed states that Jesus Christ is *homoousios* (consubstantial) with the Father—of one, identical substance with God the Father—and eternal, not created. Arius was deposed and exiled from Alexandria. Two bishops who supported him and refused to sign the creed were also deposed and exiled. There can be no question that the vast majority of the bishops came to the council already believing Jesus Christ is God incarnate, one in substance with the Father, one person of the Trinity.

The council still did not settle the controversy, however, because Arian bishops continued to agitate. They wrote letters to other bishops and to the emperor and his chaplain arguing that the creed was wrong to declare Jesus "consubstantial" with the Father. They claimed this was itself a denial of the Trinity! If God and Jesus are consubstantial, they urged, then they are one person.

The struggle over the deity of Christ and the Trinity lasted throughout most of the fourth century and only came to an end with the second ecumenical council at Constantinople in 381. Then, another emperor, sympathetic with the trinitarian bishops and the original wording of the Nicene Creed, called a council to finally settle the matter. The Council of Constantinople reaffirmed the Nicene Creed and added a third article about the Holy Spirit. With that, the doctrines of the deity of Christ and the Trinity were complete and carved in stone (so to speak).

The great champion of the Nicene Creed and of the deity of Christ and the Trinity throughout the whole controversy was Athanasius, who succeeded Alexander as bishop of Alexandria. He endured five exiles by emperors, including Constantine, for stubbornly resisting any compromises with Arianism that would have said, for example, that the Son, Jesus, is "of a similar substance" with the Father. Eventually he and his friends (known as the three "Cappadocian Fathers") prevailed. The language they used that was widely accepted is that God is "one substance and three persons." A way of saying that is "one what and three whos." They knew they were affirming a mystery, but they were not bothered by that, since God is above our finite minds' abilities to understand fully.

Nestorianism Casts Doubt on the Deity of Christ in Fifth-Century Constantinople

After the Council of Constantinople and the final writing of the Nicene Creed in 381, the vast majority of Christians throughout the Roman Empire (and beyond) believed in the full deity of Jesus. And most accepted the doctrine of the Trinity. There were, however, some exceptions. Arian missionaries in Europe had converted some of the so-called barbarian tribes to Arian Christianity. These later converted to orthodox, trinitarian Christianity. Beyond the borders of the empire it was not easy to say exactly what Christians believed. In many places they were isolated and did not participate in the doctrinal debates that led to the formal creeds of Christendom. An example is the very ancient Abyssinian Orthodox Church, the church of Ethiopia.

Within the borders of the Roman Empire, debates about the nature of Jesus Christ broke out after the Council of Constantinople. Tensions were simmering between the two main cities of the eastern, Greek-speaking half of the empire. Both Antioch and Alexandria wanted primary influence in the new capital Constantinople—where the emperors lived. Christians in those two cities had developed different approaches to theology and especially to Christology. Antioch Christians tended to emphasize Jesus's humanity and then search for an explanation of how he could also be God. Alexandria Christians tended to emphasize Jesus's deity and then search for an explanation of how he could also be human. After all, every Christian believed God and creation are radically different; how can they coexist in one person? God is infinite, eternal, and omnipotent. Above all, God is uncreated. Humanity is part of creation, even if its crown. It is finite, temporal, and limited in power. How can the uncreated and created coexist in one person?

Christian leaders were comfortable leaving this in the realm of mystery until certain Christian teachers began putting forth ideas of the person of Jesus Christ that were deeply troubling and seemed simply to repeat in fancier form earlier heresies such as adoptionism.

One major suggestion for explaining the duality of Jesus Christ, his humanity and deity, was put forward by a Christian bishop of Laodicea in Asia Minor. His name was Apollinarius and he died around 390—not long after the Council of Constantinople, which had deposed him and condemned his teaching about Christ. Jesus Christ, Apollinarius taught, was God the Son, the Word, Logos, living in a human body. The incarnation meant, he said, that the eternal Son of God took on a human body but did not really become fully and truly human. He had no human mind; his mind was God's. Some have labeled Apollinarius's heresy "God in a bod."

The Council of Constantinople considered Apollinarius's Christology a new form of docetism—the Christology of the Gnostics—that Christ only appeared to be human but was not truly human. The bishops of the council agreed with church father Gregory of Nazianzus who said "that which He [the Word] has not assumed He has not healed."[2] In other words, in order to save every part of us, the Word had to take to himself every part of us. (Sin is not "part" of us; it is simply the evilness of the will—disease or distortion and not a substance or part of humanity.)

The most vehement opposition to Apollinarius and his heresy came from Antioch, which was always seeking to protect Jesus's full and true humanity. Antioch Christians suspected that Alexandria Christians secretly sympathized with Apollinarius and his "God in a bod" heresy. They maneuvered to get one of their favorite sons elected archbishop of Constantinople—a very powerful position as it meant being the emperor's pastor! Antioch cheered when their man in Constantinople, Nestorius, was elected to that office.

One of the first things Nestorius did was preach (and publish) a sermon condemning Christians' use of the word *Theotokos* for Mary. *Theotokos* is

Greek for "God-bearer" or "Mother of God." God, Nestorius declared, cannot be born and he cannot have a mother. Mary was the "mother of Christ" (*Christotokos*) but not "mother of God."

Alexandrians in Constantinople accused Nestorius of denying the deity of Jesus Christ; and the more he defended himself, the deeper he dug the hole the Alexandrians saw him in. Eventually Nestorius began to say that Jesus was actually two persons—"The Son of God" and the "Son of David," making "Jesus Christ" a corporate personality and not one unified person. Because God-stuff (divine substance) and human-stuff (human substance) are so radically different, Nestorius argued, they cannot come together in one person. So Jesus was two natures, human and divine, and thus two persons, human and divine. The unity, he argued, lay in the absolute coordination of their wills. It was a union of wills acting as one. He even used the analogy of a perfect marriage for this special union.

Even non-Alexandrian Christians saw the problem with this. Nestorius was dividing Jesus Christ into two persons and, in effect, denying the deity of the man Jesus. How was this very different from adoptionism? Only that this was adoptionism within a trinitarian framework. Nestorius simply replaced the adopting one with the Logos (rather than the Father). The Logos, the eternal Word of God, adopted the man Jesus as his partner, so to speak, and that partnership constituted the incarnation. Only it didn't, said the critics. Being a "partner" with God does not make one God.

Nothing like the furor over Nestorianism (dividing Jesus Christ into two persons) had been seen among Christians since the controversy over Arius a century earlier. Finally a third ecumenical council met at Ephesus in Asia Minor in 431 and condemned Nestorius and his Christology. He was deposed as archbishop of Constantinople and sent into exile. But Antioch smoldered with resentment. It seemed a great triumph for Alexandria, which always emphasized Jesus's deity over his humanity.

The Council of Chalcedon Settles the Controversy over Christology

After Nestorius and his heresy were condemned in 431, another controversy broke out among Christians in Constantinople (with reverberations everywhere including Rome itself). A highly regarded monk and Christian teacher named Eutyches began attempting to refute Nestorianism (which lingered in the shadows after 431) by offering an alternative explanation of the incarnation and the person of Jesus Christ. According to him (and many in Alexandria agreed), Jesus Christ was and is a hybrid of humanity and deity—human substance and divine substance. In his view Jesus was a "third something," neither exactly human nor exactly divine. Eutyches insisted that Christ was "one nature," not two, and one person, not two. What got him into difficulty was the "one nature" language, even though it had been common in Alexandria for a long time.

The question critics (mostly from Antioch) raised is how God-stuff and human-stuff can be mixed or mingled into a third stuff. Doesn't that imply God and creation are of the same species? Doesn't that blur—if not obliterate—the line between them? Did God the Son, the Word, give up part of his deity to become human in the incarnation? Did the humanity he took on lose part of itself? Was he not, as the Nicene Creed said, "truly human and truly divine"?

Eutychianism was condemned as heresy at a fourth ecumenical council that met at Chalcedon in Asia Minor in 451. The "Chalcedonian Definition" written by the council was like an addendum to the Nicene Creed; it was never intended to be a new creed. It said that Antioch was partly right and so was Alexandria, but Antioch was also partly wrong as was Alexandria. Naturally enough, it did not satisfy extremists on either side.

Chalcedon's orthodox Christology has come to be known as the "hypostatic union"—the union of two full and complete natures, human and divine, in one unified person (*hypostasis*). In other words, Jesus Christ was and is "one who and two whats"—one undivided person but two whole natures. The Definition left this a mystery; there's no exact parallel to it anywhere in nature. The "who" of Jesus Christ is the person of the Word, the Son of God, the second person of the Trinity. The "whats" are the Son's deity and humanity brought together in him. The incarnation means that the eternal Son of God, equal with the Father, took on to himself a true human nature, not a human person.

The Chalcedonian Definition set up four "fences" to protect the mystery of the incarnation from heresies that rationalized it away. It said Jesus Christ was of two natures "without division, without separation, without mixture, without confusion." The first two "fences" were to protect the mystery of the incarnation against Nestorianism; the second two were to protect it from Eutychianism.

The hypostatic union doctrine of Chalcedon became orthodoxy from then on. During the Protestant Reformation and afterward, both Catholics and Protestants (as well as Eastern Orthodox) affirmed it. But some Christian churches in North Africa and the Middle East rejected it. Nestorian and Eutychian branches of Christianity remained separated from the church (Catholic and orthodox) for centuries. Only in the twentieth century did they rediscover each other and begin to talk again, aiming to overcome their divisions.

Modern (Live) Christological Heresies

To many laypeople and even pastors these ancient debates over the person of Jesus Christ seem esoteric, beyond comprehension, and impractical. In much of modern Christianity, "anything goes"—doctrinally. For the most part, the doctrinal orthodoxies carved out at Nicea, Constantinople, Ephesus, and Chalcedon are ignored—especially by Protestants. A few Protestant denominations remember them and continue to teach against the heresies they rejected. Because of this ignorance, all of the early Christological heresies are alive and well.

First of all, various forms of adoptionism are widely accepted in liberal Protestant theological circles. Few would say Jesus "became" divine, God's special son, only at his baptism, but many modern liberal Protestant theologians reduce Jesus Christ to a great prophet, God's "representative and deputy" among people. In the 1960s, Church of England bishop John Robinson published *Honest to God*, a popular paperback revising traditional doctrines to make them more consistent with the modern age and its worldview. Critics saw it as a radical accommodation to modern secularity. Robinson denied the supernatural entirely and argued for a new view of God's transcendence (otherness) in which God is "being itself," not a transcendent person. Later Robinson published *The Human Face of God,* a book about Jesus Christ. In it the bishop presented Jesus Christ as just a man but one who represented God perfectly.

Robinson's Christology is known as "functional Christology"—to distinguish it from "ontological Christology." The latter is that Jesus was and is actually, truly, fully human and divine in his substances. He preexisted his birth in Bethlehem as the eternal Word and Son of God and took on true humanity through Mary. He was substantially both God and human in perfect union. The former, "functional Christology," is the common view in liberal theologies that Jesus *functioned as God* but was *not God substantially*. In other words, he had no preexistence except in the mind of God. He was not literally God incarnate but a special human person who perfectly represented God to humanity. He was the paradigm of perfect God-conscious humanity. Functional Christology is the modern form of ancient adoptionism.

Arianism appears in the Christologies of several Christian sects including, most notably, the Jehovah's Witnesses (The Watchtower Bible and Tract Society). Their view of the person of Christ is that he was God's first and greatest creature, the glorious archangel Michael, who became human. Ancient Arians did not identify him with any archangel, but the contours of the two Christologies are the same—preexistence of the Word or Logos of God who is a creature, however, glorious, and incarnation into a human being. So Jesus, according to ancient and modern Arianism, was "a god" incarnate but not God incarnate. He was "a god" but not "God."

Both adoptionism and Arianism popped up among Christians throughout history. During the Reformation, a radical reformer named Faustus Socinus taught something like adoptionism. He denied the Trinity. The Reformers rejected him and his church, the Polish Brethren, a forerunner of the modern Unitarian movement. During the seventeenth and eighteenth centuries in England, many nonconformist (independent, non-Anglican) Protestants adopted Arianism as their Christology. The great poet John Milton was Unitarian as was the scientist Isaac Newton.

Apollinarianism is a common view of Jesus Christ among theologically untrained lay people. Nestorianism has not found renaissance in modern Christianity, but echoes of it can be read and heard in the teachings of some "process theologians"—Christian thinkers who adapt Christianity to the philosophy of Alfred North Whitehead. English process theologian Norman Pittenger, for example, came very close to Nestorianism in his classic book *The Word Incarnate* (1959).

Eutychianism found a home among North African Christians called monophysites. After the Council of Chalcedon, many Egyptian Christians would not sign the Chalcedonian Definition; they considered it a wholesale capitulation to Antiochian Christology with its talk of "two natures" of Christ. So most of Egyptian Christianity ("Coptic") remained faithful to Eutyches's teaching and monophysite Christology ("one nature" of Jesus—a blend of deity and humanity).

Some form of Eutychianism is common among conservative Christian laypeople. It tends to emphasize Jesus's deity at the expense of his humanity but regards him as a hybrid of human and divine—a mixture of both but not fully and truly either one. Both Apollonarianism and Eutychianism are often held unconsciously as "hunches" or "guesses" when people attempt to think about how Jesus was God incarnate.

Antidotes to Christological Heresies Ancient and Modern

Often people respond to expositions and criticisms of the ancient and modern Christological heresies with a yawn and a "So what?" Unfortunately, much modern Christianity is nondoctrinal—even when it comes to a doctrine so central to the gospel itself. I mean, of course, the incarnation—that God became human in Jesus Christ.

Too often Christianity has been reduced to a folk religion, a set of spiritual experiences and popular beliefs held without any reflection or understanding. Ancient Christianity was different. The Apostle Paul, for example, harshly criticized first-century Christians who did not teach truth and who substituted it with their own "gospels." During the great debate over the person of Christ in the late fourth century, one bishop reported that you could not go anywhere in Constantinople (and this would be true of many other cities in the Roman Empire) without being told that Christ did not have two natures or that Christ was two persons. Theology and especially Christology was on everyone's minds and tongues. Unfortunately, many times they went too far and persecuted Christians they thought held wrong beliefs. Correction—not persecution—is called for, but too often correction has gone away with persecution. Everyone's hat is his own church, so the saying goes. In other words—doctrinal anarchy: "anything goes." The church then gives an uncertain sound, like a choir singing in many keys.

The best antidote to Christological chaos is the same one recommended before about any wrong thinking in theology—understanding Christian orthodoxy and why it is what the church has taught for nearly two thousand years, and rooting it in scripture and the Great Tradition and explaining reasonably why it's superior to heresies. But first churches and individual Christians need to come to their senses about the importance of doctrine.

Without sound doctrine Christianity is reduced to individual feelings and perhaps (at best) a set of behaviors. Salvation, however, is more than right behavior; it is, according to the gospel, reconciliation with God. How does it happen? How can it happen? What has God done to make it happen? Who was and is Jesus Christ in relation to God and us? These are important and really inescapable questions once a person starts reflecting on salvation and the message about it. As the old saying goes, if we are to get the good news out, we need to get it right. Theology is all about helping us get it right.

Many people have trouble with the language of theology that developed through the controversies about Jesus Christ and the Trinity during the fourth and early fifth centuries. It seems abstract, speculative, philosophical, and removed from real discipleship. What does "hypostatic union" have to do with living the Christian life? And yet, a closer inspection of the orthodox doctrines carved out then reveals they have everything to do with salvation and Christian living. These connections are what people need to see in order to grasp the importance of orthodoxy.

The Christian gospel is not that God gave us Jesus to show us how to live; the Christian gospel is that we are helpless to live rightly and please God because of our finitude and fallenness and God has provided the solution—a perfect sacrifice for sins to make righteous his forgiveness of us. Unfortunately, many Christians past and present misunderstand the gospel and reduce it to what scholars call "moralistic therapeutic deism" (MTD). MTD is popular folk religion, not robust, "thick" Christianity. It is the idea that God is a stern, moral judge who is displeased with us but nevertheless always forgives because he's also a loving heavenly grandfather. In MTD, Jesus is God's way of telling and showing us what he expects and that he forgives when we sincerely repent. But in MTD there is no need for an incarnation or sacrifice for sins. MTD is not Christianity; it is a different religion—largely invented by people who feel guilty but also forgiven and like to think of Jesus as the model of a perfect human being. But MTD is shallow and has little to do with the New Testament or the best of Christian tradition—whether Eastern Orthodox, Roman Catholic, or Protestant. None of the great reformers would recognize it as Christian.

The real gospel, the good news that's really good, is that although we are condemned sinners, God has acted on our behalf by becoming one of us and dying for us—to reconcile us to himself and give us participation in his own divine nature (2 Pet 1:14). Where this isn't preached and taught, Christology will hardly matter. The best antidote to Christological heresies is what sociologists of religion call "thick description" of the gospel and of Christian belief throughout the ages.

What's wrong with all the Christological heresies is lack of understanding of this gospel; they all remove God from humanity and humanity from God *or* they confuse them as if they are not really so different after all. Both destroy the gospel. Orthodox Christianity has not emphasized the hypostatic union for the fun of speculation or so that intellectual theologians can lord it over ordinary people. The purpose of the hypostatic union doctrine is to preserve the gospel from destruction and protect the great mystery at the heart of God's revelation.

It is not possible to "prove" that Jesus Christ was and is God incarnate, both truly human and truly divine, one person of two natures or substances. However, in the face of denials many good arguments can be marshaled to support orthodox Christology.

First, scripture itself portrays Jesus as truly human. He needed sleep and he died. According to Luke, he grew in stature and wisdom and favor with God and people (Luke 2:52). The angels who met the disciples after Jesus's ascension told them that "this same Jesus" (a man) would return just as he left. The New Testament calls Jesus the "one mediator between God and men, the *man* Christ Jesus" (1 Tim 2:5 KJV).

Second, scripture will not allow us to worship or serve Jesus Christ as anything less than God incarnate. John 1 has already been mentioned as has the "lord, liar, or lunatic" argument of Lewis and others. The New Testament calls him "God and savior" (Titus 2:13). The disciple Thomas fell at Jesus's feet and worshipped him, calling him God (John 20:28). Jesus didn't rebuke him for it but accepted his worship.

Third, if Jesus made himself equal with God by, for example, forgiving sins and saying that if people saw him they saw the Father, then he was a blasphemer—unless he was God. His resurrection was unmistakable heavenly confirmation of his claims as true. Why would God raise a blasphemer from the dead? Why would the disciples and Paul give up their lives to martyrdom if they knew their proclamation of Jesus as Lord because of his resurrection was false?

This is Christological apologetics in a nutshell. Many, many books have written to defend the incarnation and belief that Jesus Christ was both truly God and truly human. One is *Jesus—God and Man* (1968) by German Lutheran theologian Wolfhart Pannenberg (with whom I studied).

Fourth-century Christian bishop and theologian Athanasius refuted Arianism in *On the Incarnation* ("De Incarnatione"), one of the great classics of Christian history. It's still in publication and worthy of study in Christian churches. Pope Leo I wrote a masterful defense of the hypostatic union doctrine in what has come to be known as "Leo's Tome."[3]

Evidence that this is still a living issue was provided in the 1980s when a mainline Protestant denomination struggled over whether one of its churches could call a pastor who openly denied the deity of Christ. What was once taken for granted by orthodox Christians of all denominational identities is once again disputed—mainly within mainline Protestantism (although some Catholic theologians have also questioned it)—the incarnation of God in Christ. The best antidote is a return to the gospel "once for all delivered to the saints of God" by the apostles and church discipline of ministers and leaders who doubt or deny the deity of Christ.

Bringing It Home

1. The center of Christianity is Jesus Christ. The center of conflict and controversy about Christianity is Jesus Christ. How do you understand who Jesus is and how he is both human and divine? How would you explain it to a young child or non-Christian?

2. The incarnation is a mystery of faith. United Methodist Christians affirm this in their service of Communion as found in the United Methodist hymnal where it proclaims the mystery of faith: "Christ has died; Christ has risen; Christ will come again."[4] What part does mystery play in your faith?

3. What is your reaction to the author's statement that "the Christian gospel is not that God gave us Jesus to show us how to live; the Christian gospel is that we are helpless to live rightly and please God because of our finitude and fallenness, and God has provided the solution..."?

4. If the good news is that God became one of us in order to reconcile us and give us participation in the divine nature, how could a deeper understanding of the incarnation change our mission to bring people to Jesus Christ? How could reconciliation with God and participation in the divine nature transform the world?

5. Read and discuss Luke 2:52 and 1 Timothy 2:5. What do these passages say about Jesus as both human and divine?

6. As the author reminds us, during the early centuries of Christianity, people fought and died over their convictions about who Jesus Christ is. While we are not asked to do this, after reading the chapter, why is it important that Jesus is both human and divine for your faith?

Chapter 6

Contesting the Trinity

Subordinationism, Modalism, and Tritheism

The Christian Doctrine of the Trinity

Many people, including many Christians, struggle with the doctrine of the Trinity. Commonly people describe it as that God is "one in three, three in one." That's not quite correct. The questions immediately arise "one what?" and "three what?" Are the "one" and the "three" the same? If so, then the doctrine of the Trinity contains a contradiction. Some people are okay with that, but others find that deeply troubling. Is Christian doctrine incoherent? Some regard the Trinity as the ultimate mystery—beyond comprehension. Some who consider it thus embrace it anyway and others reject it for that very reason.

Another common misconception is that the doctrine of the Trinity was invented by Christian bishops under the influence of Emperor Constantine. (This was mentioned in the previous chapter with regard to the deity of Christ.) There is a tiny bit of truth in that, but it's so incomplete as to be simply incorrect. Under Constantine and throughout the fourth century Christian bishops and leaders developed a *formal* doctrine of the Trinity—putting into new words what had always been believed by the majority of Christians. Put another way, the fourth-century fathers of the church provided a *formula* for

89

expressing the Trinity that did not exist before, but that formula said nothing so new as to distort what Christians had believed for centuries.

Another cause of misunderstanding about the Trinity and the doctrine of the Trinity is confusion of the two. In other words, the "Trinity" and the "doctrine of the Trinity" are not the same. The former is God the Father, God the Son, and God the Holy Spirit eternally existing as one God. The latter is the human formula for expressing this correctly.

I once described the doctrine of the Trinity to a class with the result that, during the discussion time that followed, a student said, "But you still haven't explained the Trinity to us." What he missed was that I was not attempting to "explain the Trinity"; that would be impossible. Can God be "explained"? No. God is transcendent and, in a sense, "wholly other." His essence is mysterious, beyond our comprehension. However, there are things we can say about God that are truer than other things. The doctrine of the Trinity is simply the Christian church's way of protecting the mystery of God from ideas about God that would destroy the mystery by overrationalizing it.

In other words, the doctrine of the Trinity can be explained; the Trinity cannot be explained. The doctrine of the Trinity was never intended to be an explanation of God; it was intended to be a model that helps people think about God in a way that does not destroy the mystery of God, is faithful to God's self-revelation in Christ, and protects God's triunity from misunderstanding and distorted explanations.

No orthodox Christians ever thought they could peer into the inner workings of Father, Son, and Holy Spirit and put together a set of words that would perfectly explain or describe their oneness and threeness. Rather, the doctrine of the Trinity is a working model, like a model of an atom or molecule, which depicts without picturing. An atom or molecule does not "look" exactly like its models, but the models scientists create help understand and work with atoms and molecules.

The doctrine of the Trinity points to a mystery but attempts to make it as intelligible as possible and ward off explanations that would distort or destroy the fullness of God's revelation of himself in Jesus Christ, the Holy Spirit, and in scripture. All the ingredients for it are found in scripture even if the words used by fourth-century theologians are more philosophical. All the ingredients for the full doctrine of the Trinity, as developed in the fourth century at Nicea and Constantinople (ecumenical councils mentioned in the previous chapter) and as explained by orthodox theologians of the time such as Cappadocian Fathers, existed in the earliest Christian writings after the New Testament. In fact, the word itself, *Trinitas*, was in use by Christians around 200.

So what is the Christian doctrine of the Trinity if not "three in one, one in three?" It was formalized and handed down to later generations of Christians during the fourth century. Its main formulators were the above-mentioned Cappadocian Fathers—Basil of Caesarea ("Basil the Great"), Gregory of Nyssa (Basil's younger brother), and Gregory of Nazianzus (their friend). They were three bishops of Asia Minor who, through their writings, helped overcome Arianism and other heresies and create an orthodox consensus about the way to express the Trinity within the Christian churches.

The Nicene Creed (written fully at the Council of Constantinople in 381) says that Father, Son (Jesus Christ), and Holy Spirit are *one in substance* ("ousia"). In other words, they are equally eternal, good, and powerful. It also says the Son, who became Jesus through the incarnation, was not created but "eternally begotten" by the Father and that the Holy Spirit eternally proceeds from the Father. (Later Western theologians and bishops added "and from the Son" but that is not in the original creed of Nicea.) The Cappadocian Fathers explained in their writings that the Father, Son, and Holy Spirit, though of the same substance and therefore equally God, are three distinct (not separate) *hypostases* (a Greek word without a good English translation). The word is usually translated "persons," but it is important to strip "persons" of all selfish individualism so that the three are not pictured as a committee. That was clearly not the church fathers' intention.

At risk of oversimplifying, here I will use a popular acrostic device to express and explain the doctrine of the Trinity (not the Trinity itself!): T.R.I.U.N.E.

In revelation, God's self-disclosure, **Three** *are represented as God*—Father, Son, and Holy Spirit. They are **regarded** *as distinct persons*. Their threeness is **immanent** *and eternal (not merely temporal)*. However, they are **united** *in essence (substance)* with **no inequality**. Finally, the doctrine of the Trinity **explains** *all doctrine but is itself inscrutable*. In other words, without it Christian beliefs (e.g., the incarnation) make no sense, but the doctrine of the Trinity is not a literal description of God who is incomprehensible in essence.

This doctrine is classical Christian belief; it is shared by all major branches of Christianity and can easily be found expressed in their books of beliefs. Its denial is why some sects that call themselves "Christian" are considered cults (in the theological sense even if they are peace-loving) by the majority of Christians. But this doctrine was carved out and into stone, so to speak, by fourth-century church fathers because some Christians were denying it. Then, before, and since. There have been three major heresies that deny the doctrine of God's triunity: subordinationism, modalism, and tritheism.

Subordinationism Challenges God's Triunity

The previous chapter discussed adoptionism and Arianism as Christological heresies. In their own ways, both deny the deity of Jesus Christ and reduce him to either a great prophet or the incarnation of an angelic being. In both cases, the person of Jesus Christ is subordinated ontologically (as to his being) to the Father. These are not views that merely subordinate the Word who became Jesus to the Father during his earthly lifetime; they subordinate him to the Father by making him a different species entirely from God—a created being, not eternal God. Why the early Christians rejected these subordinationisms was explained there.

There was and is, however, another type of subordinationism—of the Holy Spirit to God. The Holy Spirit is spoken of in scripture as both God and a distinct person—not separate from the Father and Son but distinct from them. For example, Holy Spirit is often referred to as the "Spirit of God" and plays a major role in creation and redemption. While Jesus was and is "God with us," the Holy Spirit is "God in us" by grace. Most Christians always believed this; the problem has sometimes been recognizing the Holy Spirit as a distinct person alongside Father and Son.

The problem of subordinationism of the Holy Spirit lies in depersonalizing the Spirit by depicting him/her as a force rather than as a person. (Here the pronoun used for the Spirit will be *him/her* because in the Hebrew Bible the word for God's Spirit is feminine whereas in the Greek it is neuter. There is no particular reason to think of the Spirit as more masculine than feminine. Many theologians throughout church history have recognized what Pietist theologian Ludwig Zinzendorf called "the motherly office of the Holy Spirit."[1]) Throughout church history some Christians, unfortunately, have referred to the Holy Spirit as *it* rather than as personal. This has led many Christians to think of the Holy Spirit along the lines of electricity—a power of God and not a person of the Godhead.

The New Testament, however, refers to the Holy Spirit in personal terms. Jesus promised his followers that when he left them he would send them "another comforter" or "another advocate" (the Greek is *paraclete*) to be with them and lead them into all the truth. (See especially John 14–17.) Christians are warned against grieving the Holy Spirit. There is a "sin against the Holy Spirit." The Holy Spirit spoke through prophets and descended on Jesus at his baptism in the form of a dove. All these point to the Holy Spirit as a divine person and not a force.

During the fourth century, at the same time Christians were wrestling with the deity of Christ, a group of self-proclaimed Christians denied the divinity and personality of the Holy Spirit, reducing the Spirit to a powerful presence of God at work in the world—like an emanation of God (like the rays of the sun). They were called the *pneumatomachians*—"fighters against the Holy Spirit"—by orthodox, trinitarian Christians such as the Cappadocian Fathers.

Little is known about the pneumatomachians except what their orthodox Christian opponents said. They were probably semi-Arians, heretical Christians who were willing to "compromise" with Nicene orthodoxy by altering the creed to say that the Father and the Son are "homoiousios"—of a similar substance. Of course, the Cappadocian Fathers and other orthodox trinitarian Christians saw this as no compromise at all! It would have been a complete capitulation to Arianism. Once they saw that they were not going to win the fight over the relationship of the Son with the Father, some semi-Arians probably began the struggle over the deity and personality of the Holy Spirit, arguing that the Holy Spirit is subordinate to the Father and the Son in an ontological sense. That is, according to them, the Holy Spirit is just a word for God's power. There is no third distinct personage in the Godhead.

Christians had forever believed in the deity and distinct personhood of the Holy Spirit, but there was no need to include the Holy Spirit in the Nicene Creed as the controversy was wholly about the deity of the Son. At first, the Holy Spirit didn't enter into it. But during the second half of the fourth century, the pneumatomachians launched this new offensive to stall a final formalized doctrine of the Trinity.

What was behind the Arian, semi-Arian, and pneumatomachian attacks on the Trinity? Radical monotheism known as *monarchianism*. *Monarchianism* comes from two Greek words meaning "one" and "source." Thus, monarchianism is any belief that God can be only one singular person, not two and not three, even if they share the same divine substance. So pneumatomachians were monarchians, even if they were willing temporarily to sidetrack the debate onto the subject of the Holy Spirit. Whether some of them believed in the deity of Jesus Christ is unknown but doubtful.

Pneumatomachianism, then, was subordinationism of the Holy Spirit just as Arianism was subordinationism of the Word, the Son of God. Until this controversy broke out, Christian defenders of the Trinity had not given a lot of thought to the Holy Spirit. He/she was simply assumed to be in the Godhead together with the Father and the Son. However, one of the three Cappadocian Fathers, Basil, fought the pneumatomachians by publishing the first full-length Christian treatise on the Holy Spirit entitled simply "On the Holy Spirit." There he brought out the multiple biblical texts that more than imply that the Holy Spirit is a distinct person equal with the Father and the Son. Especially useful was John 14–17. Scattered throughout those chapters are numerous references to the Spirit (in Jesus's own words) that cannot be understood as referring to an impersonal power or force. In Jesus's teaching, the Holy Spirit is his own alter ego and yet distinct. He/she is sent by the Father and given to the disciples by Jesus to teach and guide them and to be their advocate.

The second ecumenical council at Constantinople in 381 added the "third article" about the Holy Spirit to the creed. From then on it has been considered orthodox to believe in the Holy Spirit as equally divine with Father and Son and as a distinct person within God just as the Word, Jesus, is a distinct person within God.

Here a question naturally arises that has bedeviled orthodox Christians for centuries: Does the Holy Spirit proceed eternally from the Father only or also from the Son? As mentioned before, the Western, Latin-speaking churches (Roman Catholic and Protestant) added to the Nicene Creed that the Holy Spirit proceeds from the Father *and the Son* ("filioque"). The Eastern Orthodox churches reject that addition, arguing it subordinates the Holy Spirit to the Son. And yet the Eastern churches all believe in and teach the "monarchy of the Father"—that the Father is the "source of divinity" of the Son and Holy Spirit—eternally without beginning. Just as the warmth and heat of the sun are of its own substance and yet proceed from it, so the Son and Spirit are of the Father's substance and yet proceed from him.

Subordinationism does not mean belief that the Father is the source of the Son and Spirit; it means that the Son and Spirit are created and not

94

equal with the Father in substance, especially that they are not eternal. It is orthodox, even if disputed, to believe that the Father is the Son's and Spirit's source.

Modalism Reduces the Trinity to Oneness

One of the most popular analogies for the Trinity, often used by Sunday school teachers and youth leaders, is *water*. Water is a single substance (H_2O) but it can take three forms—solid (ice), liquid (water), and vapor (steam). So, the analogy goes, the Father, Son, and Holy Spirit are simply three forms or manifestations of the one divine substance that God is. This is the heresy called "modalism." In early Christian literature and in some technical books of theology it is also sometimes called "Sabellianism" (after an early Christian who taught it) or "Patripassionism" (from two Latin words that mean "Father" and "suffering").

The essence of modalism is that Father, Son, and Holy Spirit are not in any sense "persons" but merely outward manifestations of the one God-person. Some early Christians who adopted this idea found it easy to communicate the Trinity (wrongly) to inquirers by pointing to the Greek theatre in which one actor played many roles by wearing different masks. The Greek word for *mask* could also be used for "person," so "three persons of God" simply meant (to the modalists) three masks that God wears in history—sometimes appearing on history's "stage" as Father, sometimes as Son (Jesus), and sometimes as Holy Spirit. But behind the masks or manifestations (modes) is one person.

Again, the motive for modalism was monarchianism. This is called "modalistic monarchianism" because it, too, begins with the assumption that monotheism must mean God can be only one person in undifferentiated unity. Any distinctions must be in appearance only. Thus, to the modalists, the triunity of God is not *immanent* (within God himself) but only *economic* (outward).

Again, one of the Cappadocian Fathers, this time Gregory of Nyssa, Basil's younger brother, wrote the definitive treatise exposing modalism as wrong: *On Not Three Gods*. The modalistic monarchians were claiming that the doctrine of the Trinity represented God as three gods—polytheism. Gregory demonstrated how that is not true. God is only one being but with inner differentiation. Some of Basil's arguments are biblical and some more philosophical in nature, but together they show that modalism is really impossible if one believes in the Bible and that God is love.

If God is one person and his essence is love, whom did God love before he created anything? According to Gregory and other antimodalist, orthodox Christians, modalism makes the world necessary to God—as God's counterpart, something to love. This detracts from God's glorious otherness, his freedom and power.

If God is one person and the three are only outward modes or manifestations, did Jesus project his voice into heaven at his baptism when the Father spoke and said, "This is my Son whom I dearly love" (Matt 3:17)? What was the Spirit who descended like a dove? To whom was Jesus speaking when he said on the cross, "Father, *into your hands I entrust my life*" (Luke 23:46)? How could the Spirit be "another advocate" Jesus promised to send to his disciples? To whom was Jesus speaking in the garden when he prayed to the Father, "Not my will but your will must be done" (Luke 22:42)? It is impossible to square modalism with the biblical narrative.

Finally, if God is one person and not Father, Son, or Holy Spirit (these being masks God wears), then who is God? What person is he? Wouldn't this mean that God's revelation does not reveal but hides him? If modalism is true, then God is someone lurking hidden behind the masks who is never really revealed.

These and other arguments against modalism were used by church fathers to support orthodox belief that Father, Son, and Holy Spirit are not mere modes or manifestations of God but real, distinct persons. But doesn't that imply three gods? It would if we projected onto "person" modern American ideas. Our individualist culture defines "person" as "separate self." People say of a toddler that "she's becoming her own person" when she says "no" and "mine." We think of persons as over against each other in self-differentiation. I am a person only to the extent that I stand out, apart. A children's book author has one of his characters say to a boy, "Your job is not to fit in but to stand out!" That is our modern, American notion of "person." It was *not* the ancient idea of person nor is it the idea of person in most cultures of the world.

Saying that God is three persons implies tritheism, three gods, *only* if we project onto Father, Son, and Spirit our modern, distorted ideas of persons as individual selves. If we realize that to be a person is to fit in rather than stand out, as most cultures in the world do, then tritheism is not as much of a threat. But also we need to remember that when the early orthodox Christians called God "three persons" they were simply using the closest word they could come up with for something that is ultimately mysterious. Fifth-century church father Augustine said that we do not say "three persons" because we want to but only because we have no alternative.

Many people were and are modalists in their thinking about the Trinity because they cannot picture three persons as anything but a committee or even dysfunctional family. "Committee" is the worst analogy for the threeness of God! Family might be a good analogy if it could be stripped of all dysfunction and inequality.

Is modalism really a heresy or just a misunderstanding caused by mental confusion? It depends on who is thinking it. If someone understands the orthodox doctrine of the Trinity and rejects it in favor of modalism, that is heresy. If someone adopts modalism just because he cannot wrap his mind around the orthodox doctrine and is confused, that is not heresy, just confusion. Most modern modalists are probably just confused.

Tritheism Distorts the Trinity into Polytheism

Tritheism is the belief that Father, Son, and Holy Spirit are three different gods—a Christian form of polytheism. Fortunately, very few, if any, Christians have ever believed that—at least not consciously or willfully. On the other hand, some Christian theologians and teachers of doctrine have been accused of falling into tritheism accidentally or implicitly. And many theologians suspect that many Christians *think* of the Trinity in ways that imply tritheism. If anyone actually used the "committee analogy" for the Trinity, that would be tritheism.

The main challenges to belief in the Trinity in ancient Christianity were monarchian. Almost all its opponents claimed it led inevitably to tritheism. Yet, so long as you affirm that Father, Son, and Holy Spirit are three distinct persons sharing equally and eternally the same substance, you are trinitarian *even if* you go on to explain or express the Trinity in ways that *seem* tritheistic. So, among orthodox Christians, tritheism hardly exists except as a warning: "Be careful how you say that; you might mislead people to think of the Trinity tritheistically." Or as a criticism: "That theologian accidently fell into tritheism when he said that about the Trinity."

The point is that it is almost impossible to find any person claiming to be a Christian, ancient or modern, who actually said or says that Father, Son, and Holy Spirit are three different gods.

One has to dig deep into ancient Christianity to find hidden, unconscious tritheism. Gregory of Nyssa, in spite of being a champion of trinitarian orthodoxy, used one analogy (in *On Not Three Gods*) that *could be* and *was* accused of being tritheistic. He argued that Jesus's disciples Peter, James, and John shared the same substance—humanity—and therefore could be a dim analogy of the Trinity. However, he used other analogies that balanced that, emphasizing the oneness of Father, Son, and Holy Spirit. All images and analogies have problems; each one inclines toward some heresy and all must be balanced with other analogies to provide balance.

During the Middle Ages, a Christian theologian named Joachim of Fiore (or sometimes "Flora") was at the center of a group of thinkers who attempted to reemphasize the threeness of God. They believed the Western churches, under the influence of Augustine, had wandered away from God's threeness into an unbalanced emphasis on God's oneness—a kind of implicit monarchianism. However, to most catholic and orthodox Christians' way of thinking, Joachim and his circle of theologians fell into tritheism by describing Father, Son, and Holy Spirit as different persons presiding over and revealing God in different eras of history. Joachim envisioned a coming "Age of the Spirit" that would be a new "dispensation" of God in relation to the world.

A problem here is that it's easy to confuse the immanent and economic modes of the Trinity and difficult to tell which a theologian such as Joachim is talking about. The "immanent Trinity" is Father, Son, and Holy Spirit in themselves in eternity apart from the world. The "economic Trinity" is Father, Son, and Holy Spirit in relation to the world "dispensing" the benefits of creation and redemption. The former is eternal and the latter is temporal. Was Joachim (and theologians under his influence) talking about Father, Son, and Holy Spirit *economically* or *immanently*? If the latter, then tritheism seems to be a danger. If only the former, then the differences he described between Father, Son, and Holy Spirit are only in the "economy"—God's action in relation to the world. That would not imply tritheism unless he pitted them against each other, which he did not. The charge against Joachim (and others) that they fell into tritheism is much debated. The Catholic Church of his day said he did and condemned his teaching as heresy. Many later theologians think that was a mistake based on a misunderstanding. Nowhere did Joachim or others say that Father, Son, and Holy Spirit are different gods.

One thing is clear from the Bible and the Great Tradition of Christian orthodoxy—tritheism is wrong and a danger to be avoided. Exactly what counts as tritheism is not as clear. Not all theologians who use the so-called "social analogy" of the Trinity are guilty of tritheism, but they often are accused of it anyway. (The "social analogy" is comparing the triunity of God to a human community such as family but stripped of all inequalities and dysfunctions.)

Modern Forms of Trinitarian Heresies

Blatant trinitarian heresy exists outside orthodox Christianity; among orthodox Christians it is never blatant but the result of misunderstanding and confusion.

Subordinationism of the Son and the Holy Spirit is the "orthodoxy" of several offshoots of the Adventist movement of the nineteenth century. (Seventh-day Adventists are orthodox, however.) The Jehovah's Witnesses teach subordinationism. To them the Son and the Spirit are not equal with the Father, "Jehovah," who alone is God. The Son is a heavenly creature who become human as Jesus and the Spirit is a power of God, not a person.

As mentioned in the previous chapter, some liberal Christian theologians have fallen into subordinationism through various types of functional Christology—reducing Jesus Christ to a great prophet, model of true humanity, representative, and deputy of God, and so on. That makes a robust orthodox doctrine of the Trinity impossible. Unfortunately many denominations have been relaxed about allowing that in the ranks of their ministers and theologians.

Modalism is the primary modern heresy about the Trinity; it's common, even rampant. Only one organized group of Christians actually holds modalism as its official doctrine of God, however, and they are called "Oneness Pentecostals" or "Jesus Only" Christians. Two large denominations exist— one primarily Caucasian and one primarily African-American. The United Pentecostal Church (and churches once affiliated with it) and the Pentecostal Assemblies of the World teach a modalistic doctrine of the Trinity—that Father, Son, and Holy Spirit are simply three "names" and "manifestations" of the person Jesus or that *Jesus* is the one name of the three forms of God known in the Bible as Father, Son, and Holy Spirit. (I have talked with Oneness Pentecostals who say it both ways.) Many Oneness Pentecostal churches are called "Apostolic," but there are other groups that share that moniker that are not modalistic. Trinitarian Pentecostals such as the Assemblies of God and the Church of God in Christ tend to shun the Oneness Pentecostals and the latter return the favor. This has been *the* major division among Pentecostals for over a century.

One of the best-known and most influential preachers in America and around the world is T. D. Jakes, pastor of Potter's House, a megachurch in Dallas, Texas. Although he and his church (and its many offshoots) are not officially united with either Oneness Pentecostal denomination, Jakes has often used modalistic language of Father, Son, and Holy Spirit as "manifestations" of God. This has led many critics to accuse him of modalism, but Jakes has responded to them by saying that he now accepts the orthodox doctrine of the Trinity. Nevertheless, to the extent that Jakes still uses the term *manifestations* for Father, Son, and Holy Spirit his language is more modalistic than orthodox.

The largest presence of modalism, however, is probably in the minds of many ordinary Christian members of orthodox churches. When one listens to them talk about the Trinity modalistic language and illustrations abound. This is just confusion, not heresy. In fact, some orthodox Christians think most modalists are just confused—even Oneness Pentecostals!

Again, tritheism is difficult to find in any explicit, blatant form. Like unconscious modalism, it creeps into everyday Christian language through confusion and lack of precision. Some Christians who talk about the "eternal councils of the Godhead" seem to think of the Trinity as a heavenly committee, which would be heresy if it were actually embraced and taught. In most cases it's just a result of not being taught better.

However, many orthodox believers have detected tritheism in the teaching of the Church of Jesus Christ of Latter-day Saints (Mormons) whose official statement of faith describes Father, Son, and Holy Spirit as "three separate divine personages." Father and Son are said to be male beings of the same species as humans. The Holy Spirit is said to be a nonbodily spiritual being. The problem with calling this tritheism is that it exists within a larger doctrine of gods in which there is no one, supreme God over all but "gods many." (Exactly what constitutes official Mormon doctrine is not always easy to say, but the plurality of gods has been stated by church presidents who are supposed to be prophets.) However, I know Mormon teachers of doctrine who do *not* believe that but instead affirm that the Father of Jesus Christ is eternal God over all, maker of heaven and earth and everything outside of himself and that Jesus Christ is the incarnation of the eternal Son of God. The only conclusion is that the Church of Jesus Christ of Latter-day Saints is large enough to allow diversity of belief within its ranks. It does appear to outsiders, however, that the official teaching of the church is tritheistic if not blatantly polytheistic (many gods). A careful, biblical, orthodox trinitarian would never say that Father, Son, and Holy Spirit are "three separate divine personages." They are *distinct* but never *separate*.

Only one orthodox modern theologian I know of has been accused of blatant tritheism—German theologian Jürgen Moltmann. In his classic work *The Crucified God* (1974), Moltmann described the cross of Jesus Christ as a "stasis" within God—"God against God"—because of Jesus's "cry of dereliction": "My God, my God, why have you left me?" (Matt 27:46). He argued that this was not just Jesus's emotional feeling, abandonment by God, but an actual event within God—self-abandonment. In a later book, *The Trinity and the Kingdom of God* (1981), the German theologian described the unity of God as eschatological—future—and made it sound as if during history God is somewhat divided. He specifically appealed to the theology of Joachim as a model, but Moltmann embraced the idea that the "economic Trinity is the immanent Trinity" so that it would be difficult to give him the same benefit of the doubt. In other words, for Moltmann, whatever is happening between Father, Son, and Holy Spirit in the history of the world (economic Trinity) is happening within God himself (immanent Trinity).

These trinitarian speculations have brought on Moltmann the frequent charge of tritheism, and yet he denies it and it's usually believed that tritheism is not his intention. He does not believe in "three gods." For him, the love shared equally by Father, Son, and Holy Spirit binds them together as one God so that, ultimately, there can be no real division or separation among them. Still, the shadow of tritheism lingers over Moltmann's whole theological project.

Antidotes to Trinitarian Heresies

Correct theology is informed by four sources: scripture, tradition, reason, and experience. The best antidote to trinitarian heresies, as to all heresies, is for pastors and other Christians leaders to teach the orthodox doctrine of the Trinity showing its roots in scripture and tradition and its consistency with reason and experience. Simply saying that "we believe" God is "three in one and one in three" is no help and may, in fact, be worse than saying nothing. But the latter isn't helpful, either. I was once a member of a church with the word *Trinity* in its name for eight years and never once heard a sermon, Sunday school lesson, or Bible study on the doctrine of the Trinity. I am almost certain the majority of church members knew little or nothing about the doctrine of the Trinity. That opens the door to trinitarian heresies that abound in the theologically untrained minds of Christian laypeople as well as in non-Christian sects that claim to be Christian. The list of books at the end of this chapter will help pastors and other Christian leaders as well as laypeople interested in understanding the doctrine of the Trinity.

The very best antidote to trinitarian heresies, of course, is scripture itself. Here, in the remainder of this chapter, each trinitarian heresy will be taken apart using scripture above all, but mention will be made also of tradition, reason, and experience as antidotes.

Subordinationism of the Son and the Holy Spirit to the Father is falsified by scripture. Again, however, *subordinationism* does not mean just "the monarchy of the Father" within the Trinity (an orthodox doctrine) or the subordination of the persons of the Trinity to one another in the economic Trinity—the Trinity in salvation history. Subordinationism *always* means belief that *only* the Father is God; the Son and Spirit are not truly God but creatures or (in the case of the Spirit) an impersonal power or force of God.

Biblical reasons for rejecting subordinationism have already been provided, but more can be said. In John 17, Jesus prayed to the Father, "Glorify me with the glory we shared before the world began" (my translation of verse 5). God's "glory" is God's alone; God does not "share" his glory with another. Acts 5 tells the story of two early Christians who are said to have lied to the Holy Spirit. Then it says they lied not to "men" but to "God." The chapter clearly intends readers to understand that lying to the Holy Spirit *is* lying to God. The two are the same.

These are just a couple examples of antisubordinationist scripture passages that point clearly to the Trinity. In fact, they cannot be understood any other way.

What about tradition? All major branches of Christianity have always insisted on the full, robust doctrine of the Trinity as essential for Christianity.

Churches and individual teachers who deny the Trinity have always been excluded from ecumenical Christian groups—at least until the rise of liberal theology in the modern world. Still, even to this day, Unitarian churches, which deny the Trinity, are generally excluded from even the most inclusive ecumenical groups of churches and ministers.

Reason and Christian experience (worship) support trinitarian belief. If God is love and not in some sense a community of persons then whom did God love before the world began? How could God be personal without relationships? Denial of the Trinity leads either to belief that the world is somehow necessary to God or that God is not essentially loving and his act of creation was a whim, not an expression of love. Christian worship has always been trinitarian. Worshipping Jesus as God was common, even universal, among earliest Christians as anti-Christian orator and writer Celsus revealed.

What about modalism? At least it affirms that Jesus, the Son of God, and the Holy Spirit are God and not creatures. Modalists worship Jesus as God and believe the Holy Spirit is God in them. In my opinion, this does set them apart from subordinationists who deny the deity of Christ and the person-hood of the Holy Spirit. After many long talks with self-professed modalist Christians (mostly "Apostolic Pentecostals") I am convinced the source of their adherence to modalism is confusion about the doctrine of the Trinity. They have been convinced that the orthodox doctrine of the Trinity is trithe-ism or polytheism. They simply do not understand the oneness of God in orthodox trinitarianism or it is not expressed strongly enough for them. But they also tend to overlook or have trouble explaining the many scripture pas-sages in which Father, Son, and Holy Spirit are distinguished from each other (as mentioned earlier).

As hinted before, a key antidote to modalism is for trinitarian Christians to remember and explain carefully that "persons" (in the doctrine of the Trinity) does *not* mean "individual selves over against each other"—the mod-ern American idea of "person." Many people adopt or defend modalism sim-ply because they misunderstand the "three persons" language to imply that Father, Son, and Holy Spirit are three persons *in the same sense* as three human persons.

Another antidote to modalism is to point out to modalists or those at-tracted to it that it's simply inconsistent with the biblical narrative that in many instances clearly portrays Father, Son, and Holy Spirit as three distinct persons, not merely modes or manifestations of one person. Examples were given above. Also, *if* modalism is true, then God's revelation of himself as Father, Son, and Holy Spirit is not "revelation of God" at all; it is a hiding of God behind three "masks." Who *God* actually is is left unknown if Father, Son, and Holy Spirit are not real distinctions within God.

An antidote to tritheism is a proper emphasis on what the ancient Christians called the "perichoresis" of Father, Son, and Holy Spirit—their interdependence and interpenetration. They indwell each other in such a strong bond of unity that together they are one God—not at all like a committee or even a dysfunctional family. Some lay Christians especially need to be reminded that there is no need to parcel out worship and devotion equally to Father, Son, and Holy Spirit as if any one of them would feel slighted if he/she got more attention than the others. Worship of the Father is exactly what the Son Jesus wants from us. Worship of Jesus is what the Holy Spirit wants (as well as worship of the Father). Father and Son want us to glorify and worship the Holy Spirit. There's *no competition* between them.

Bringing It Home

1. Discuss the distinction between the Trinity and the doctrine of the Trinity.

2. In the doctrine of the Trinity, the Church provides a *formula*. The purpose is to protect the mystery of God and be faithful to God's self-revelation in Christ without distortion. So language about the Trinity can only be an approximation and never a complete description. What are some ways that language can both reveal and yet hide meaning?

3. Reread the author's acrostic to express and explain the doctrine of the Trinity: "In revelation, God's self-disclosure, **Three** are represented as God—Father, Son, and Holy Spirit. They are **regarded** as distinct persons. Their threeness is **immanent** *and eternal (not merely temporal).* However, they are **united** *in essence (substance)* with **no inequality**. Finally, the doctrine of the Trinity **explains** *all doctrine but is itself inscrutable.*" Discuss how the Trinity is not three gods.

4. The author says that without the doctrine of the Trinity other Christian beliefs make no sense. Other than the incarnation,

what other beliefs would not make sense if not for the doctrine of the Trinity?

5. Discuss John 14–17. What do these biblical passages say about the Holy Spirit? What is wrong with the analogy of water for describing the Trinity? What analogy might work better?

Good Books about the Trinity

Byassee, Jason. *Trinity: The God We Don't Know* (Nashville: Abingdon Press, 2015).

Castelo, Daniel. *Confessing the Triune God* (Eugene, OR: Cascade Books, 2014).

Hall, Christopher, and Roger E. Olson. *The Trinity* (Grand Rapids: Eerdmans, 2002).

Macchia, Frank D. *The Trinity, Practically Speaking* (Downers Grove, IL: InterVarsity Press, 2010).

Moltmann, Jürgen. *The Crucified God* (Minneapolis: Fortress, 1993).

———. *The Trinity and the Kingdom* (Minneapolis: Fortress, 1993).

Peters, Ted. *God as Trinity: Relationality and Temporality in Divine Life* (Louisville: Westminster John Knox, 1993).

Chapter 7

Setting Grace Aside
Pelagianism and Semi-Pelagianism

Christianity a Religion of Grace Alone

Most Christians are at least aware of the keystone passage about salvation in Ephesians 2:8-9: "You are saved by God's grace because of your faith. This salvation is God's gift. It's not something you possessed. It's not something you did that you can be proud of." Over the Christian centuries this and other clear biblical passages have given weight to an orthodox consensus that salvation is wholly God's doing and not at all earned by humans; it is sheer, undeserved grace. Now this doesn't mean that all Christians have ever agreed about a secondary issue—whether human persons can and must cooperate with grace by freely receiving it or whether even their reception of saving grace is God's doing. We'll look into that debate among orthodox Christians briefly, but here the main emphasis is on the Christian orthodox consensus—that God alone saves and that even the beginning of a good will toward God is enabled by God's grace and not solely a human achievement.

Some may wonder whether I'm here only describing *Protestant* doctrine. Many Protestants and not a few Catholics think Catholic theology says people must earn grace through faith "and good works." That's complicated by some Catholic language (e.g., "merit") but, basically, no; Catholic teaching is that *salvation is by grace alone through faith and works of love.* In other words,

106

with Protestants (and Eastern Orthodox) Catholics believe God does all the saving, allowing humans to cooperate with faithfulness to the sacraments and good works. But even their cooperation is enabled by grace and not something even saints can boast about.

This is one area of Christian doctrine widely misunderstood by especially (but not only) American Christians. Popular folk religious sayings such as "God helps those who help themselves" and the American penchant for "pulling ourselves up by our bootstraps" have contributed to a kind of default American heresy—that salvation is half God's work and half ours. Or at least that God waits for us to initiate a saving relationship with him and then he responds. As we will see, that's a heresy called "semi-Pelagianism." More on that later.

Someone may be thinking of another scripture passage besides Ephesians 2:8-9. Philippians 2:12b-13 says, "Continue to work out your salvation with fear and trembling, for it is God who works in you to will and to act in order to fulfill his good purpose" (NIV). Doesn't this say that salvation is something we human beings must work on, even contribute to? Actually, English translations of this passage can mislead from its true meaning. The Greek is clearer. In verse 12, the English word *work* translates the Greek word *katergezesthe*, which means "carry on to completion." In verse 13, the English word *work* translates the Greek word *energon*, which means "provides all the ability." In other words, studied in the original language, the passage that many people think teaches partial works salvation actually does not; it teaches that even our activity in spiritual growth is wholly enabled by God. Again, salvation is all of grace.

During the Protestant Reformation, the reformers Martin Luther, Ulrich Zwingli, John Calvin, and others wished to downplay good works as contributing anything to salvation, so they promoted the doctrine that salvation is "by grace alone through faith alone." "Faith alone" is contrary to Catholic teaching, but "grace alone" is not. The debate was about whether the saving grace of God was received by faith (trust) alone or by faith plus works of love—"good works." In either case, however, reconciliation with God and a strong relationship with God is a bridge built from God's side; all we have to do is walk across it and even our ability to do that is enabled by God's grace. So, in technical theological language, Catholics, Orthodox, and Protestants have always agreed (in spite of often seeming not to!) that God's grace is the efficient cause of salvation while faith is the primary instrumental cause of salvation. Whether works of love are necessary as co-instruments of salvation is where Catholics and Protestants have traditionally disagreed. Eastern Orthodox Christians side with Catholics about that.

In spite of that divide among orthodox Christians, however, all agree that no part of salvation is earned by human persons in such a way that forces grace or allows the saved sinner to boast. All agree that good works flow from reconciliation with God and are its products, not what produces it. All agree that good works are necessary—as evidences of a saved life. Grace runs throughout all branches of classical, orthodox Christianity and groups that make salvation depend partly on autonomous good works (good works achieved independently of grace) are generally considered sects or cults on the margins of Christianity if not totally away from it.

None of this is to say that some average Christians fully realize this emphasis on grace alone and never fall into confusion about grace and good works. Surely many do. But that is different from a self-identified Christian leader or teacher who knows what the Christian consensus has always been and goes against it by emphasizing the power of sinful human persons to contribute to their salvation without the help of grace.

Some readers may wonder about the great founder of Methodism (and its offshoots), John Wesley. Lutheran and Reformed (Calvinist) Protestants have often singled out Wesley and Methodists for defecting from belief in salvation by grace alone through faith alone. It's true that Wesley emphasized good works—but only as the necessary fruit of a born-again Christian life. His writings on "justification" (initial reconciliation with God, forgiveness, and right standing with God) clearly agree with Luther and Calvin that it is by grace alone through faith alone. However, he strongly believed and taught that humans have free will to either resist or cooperate with God's grace (synergism) while Luther and Calvin believed they do not and that God alone does all the saving without human cooperation (monergism). Still and nevertheless, Wesley and all his faithful Methodist followers (including many who do not use the label *Methodist*) insisted that if a person is "saved" it is solely God's doing and not at all an autonomous human achievement through good works. For him and them, good works flow naturally from a life saved by the grace of God through faith alone.

To a certain extent this whole divide among orthodox Christians comes down to this: Is salvation by grace alone through faith *as trust* alone, or is salvation by grace through faith understood as *trust and obedience*—that is, "faithfulness" to the way of Jesus Christ? For all their differences, Wesley, orthodox

Christians, and Catholics take the second view while Luther, Calvin, and all their followers take the first view. But even Wesley, orthodox Christians, and Catholics have never believed or taught that humans achieve salvation apart from God's grace. Rather, for them as for Luther and Calvin, grace is the sole cause of salvation even if faithfulness is necessary to keep salvation.

So what exactly is the Christian doctrinal consensus about salvation? Well, put most simply, it is that *if a person is saved it has nothing to do with his or her goodness but only to do with God's grace.* Grace is the sole efficient cause of salvation. Salvation is sheer gift.

So what is *grace*? From a Christian perspective, grace is God's "undeserved favor." "Prevenient grace" is God's undeserved enabling power to hear, understand, and receive salvation offered freely by God through Christ. It is grace that goes before human decision and reception (repentance and faith). It is grace that calls, convicts, illumines, and enables. "Saving grace" is God's embrace in reconciliation. Exactly when that first happens is much disputed among Christians. Is it at baptism or at conversion or somehow both? Either way, God's acceptance of a sinner as right with him, forgiven, and in his fellowship is "salvation," and it cannot be earned. It is God's mercy alone.

The Heresy of Self-Salvation: Pelagianism

The doctrine of salvation is another one where heresy is the mother of orthodoxy. However, as implied in previous chapters, we must distinguish between *implicit* and *explicit* orthodoxy. The former is what was already taught and believed by Christians following the apostles *before* there was need to put it down in some official way. The latter is the formal, official expression of the former. So, the "hypostatic union" doctrine of the person of Christ was the explicit orthodoxy prefigured in the implicit common belief that Jesus is God incarnate and therefore human and divine. Long before certain heresies arose that challenged biblical teaching about salvation through grace alone, the vast majority of Christian thinkers and leaders embraced it. A problem is that during the second century and afterward *some* orthodox Christians tended to emphasize good works and holy living because the Gnostics believed they were not important. If salvation is purely spiritual and has nothing to do with a body that is the seat of sin, as some Gnostics taught, then what you do with the body is unimportant. Some Gnostics fell into rank immorality to prove

109

their salvation was independent of their bodies. Against this "antinomian" (against law) heresy, many early church fathers stressed the importance of good works and holy living for authentic Christianity. That, in turn, led some orthodox Christians to become legalistic about salvation and require strict asceticism for full salvation. Some even went so far as the castrate themselves.

Still and nevertheless, all the church fathers emphasized that salvation is God's work alone and that it is enabled by grace such that sinners cannot contribute anything to their own salvation; they can only freely accept it by faith and demonstrate it through acts of love.

Augustine, bishop of Hippo in North Africa, was the dominant Christian theologian in the West (Latin-speaking half of the Roman Empire) in the first third of the fifth century. He experienced a dramatic conversion from paganism to Christianity and in his *Confessions* attributed it solely to God's grace. According to him, not only his own salvation but everyone's is an act of God on behalf of and within him and them. Augustine emphasized monergism (God as the sole actor in salvation) and the passivity of sinners being saved. He allowed synergism in Christian life, but not in initial salvation. The Christian life consists of faith and good works, but salvation, one's relationship with God as forgiven and considered righteous, is solely by grace. Every truly good thing a person has or does is a gift of God, according to Augustine.

Augustine believed the Bible teaches that before and apart from God's supernatural grace all human beings, including infants, are damned sinners capable only of evil. That's because of inherited sin. Every human person, he taught, inherits Adam's guilt and corruption of nature. Before Adam rebelled against God he was capable of either sinning or not sinning. Afterward, however, he and all his posterity are capable only of sinning—without the supernatural grace of God. Even after a person is saved, Augustine preached, every good achievement *in the spiritual realm* is God working in and through the person. All credit and glory for goodness go to God alone.

Eastern (Greek-speaking) Christians of Augustine's time were not of the same opinion about the human condition. Eastern Orthodox Christians still do not believe in "total depravity." However, the majority of Eastern church fathers of Augustine's time (e.g., the Cappadocian Fathers) agreed that salvation is solely by the grace of God and not something anyone can earn. Augustine based his strong view of human depravity on passages such as Psalm 14 and Romans 1. He based his strong view of God's grace on passages such as Romans 3 and 9 and on verses such as 1 Corinthians 4:7b: "What do you have that you didn't receive? And if you received it, then why are you bragging as if you didn't receive it?" But above all Augustine based his strong emphasis on grace on the cross of Jesus Christ: Why would Jesus have died for all if some can save themselves through good works?

One of Augustine's favorite prayers was, "O, God, command whatever you will, but give what you command." This was his way of expressing his belief that God gives every perfect gift including the ability to keep his commandments. We are incapable of obeying God without God's supernatural help (grace). Some Christians in Rome and elsewhere misunderstood and misused Augustine's prayer. They said that God had not given the gift of chastity yet, so they were incapable of obeying God's command to avoid immorality. It was God's fault they sinned! Of course, Augustine intended no such thing, but some Christians distorted his teaching in that manner to justify their sinful lifestyles.

A particularly strict monk from Britain named Pelagius visited Rome in the early fifth century. He noticed that many Christians were living immoral lives and justifying that by quoting Augustine. He began to read Augustine's books and found that he strongly disagreed. So he began to preach in Rome and everywhere he traveled that people are capable of obeying God *on their own without any special help from God's grace* and that sin is never necessary or inevitable in human life. God's grace is his giving of the law to show us how to please him and his forgiveness when we truly repent for having disobeyed him. But, the ideal, Pelagius taught, is to live such a perfectly holy life of obedience to God's will that one never has to repent at all! And that's not an impossible ideal; it's fully possible in our natural state.

Pelagius rejected the whole idea of original sin—except as bad examples set by others that seduce us to sin. There is, he taught, no inherited sinfulness—either as guilt or corruption of nature. Each and every human is born into this world exactly as Adam was created—capable of hearing and obeying God and living in fellowship with him from beginning to end. That most do not is not due to original sin but choice.

Pelagius wrote a book against Augustine's view of original sin, total depravity, and human dependence on grace entitled *On Nature*. There he argued, on the basis of free will (which Augustine had affirmed in his *Confessions*) and responsibility, that all humans need is moral guidance toward the good, not supernatural help to do the good. He affirmed prevenient grace but only as

God's gracious provision of the law. Original sin, he argued, is only the bad examples of sinners who influence us—a social "weight" of sinful influence.

Augustine reacted almost violently to Pelagius's book. He responded with his own book entitled *On Nature and Grace* in which he spelled out his own doctrine of original sin and human depravity and argued that nobody except Jesus (because he was conceived without original sin) is capable of obeying God without the special aid of grace. Above all he insisted that salvation itself is totally dependent on the cross of Christ and God's grace through faith and the sacraments. (But he averred that the sacrament of baptism "works" to convey grace "ex opera operato"—apart from faith.)

So vicious was Augustine's response to Pelagius that the British monk fled Rome, where Augustine's influence was strong, to the East where he hoped to find a more favorable hearing among Greek-speaking Christians. Augustine wrote ahead to his friend Jerome, who lived in Palestine, and urged him to spread the news that Pelagius was a heretic. When Pelagius arrived in the East, he received a chilly reception but not outright rejection. He was granted hearings by several gatherings of bishops and seemed to contradict himself under close questioning. For example, he defended himself by saying that he never claimed anyone actually *does* perfectly obey God but only that it is possible.

Eventually Pelagius and his denial of original sin and total dependence on God's supernatural grace was condemned by the third ecumenical council at Ephesus—the same one that condemned Nestorius and his teaching about the person of Christ (as really two persons). Pelagius was sent into exile by the emperor. From there he spent the rest of his life writing books and letters to defend his theology of sin and salvation, but he was largely ignored.

As in the case of other heretics we have encountered, it's not entirely possible to know with certainty exactly what Pelagius's teaching was. First, his books (two whose titles are known) are lost. The only record we have of them is extensive quotations in Augustine's and other anti-Pelagians' writings. (It is possible that all of Pelagius's *On Nature* is contained in *On Nature and Grace*, but there is no way to be certain of that or that Augustine quoted it fairly—although most scholars suppose so.) Second, Pelagius altered his teaching considerably as he was subjected to withering interrogation by bishops—especially in the East where he received a more favorable reception than in the West where Augustine reigned. He seems to have accommodated his view to theirs.

So, what matters is not so much what Pelagius himself taught as the heresy that bears his name—whether deservedly so or not. There can be little question that some ancient Christians believed something like what Pelagius taught. If not, the Council of Ephesus would have had little reason to be concerned. What the Council said was that it is *not possible not to sin* due to Adam's fall and our inheritance of its corruption (it left aside the issue of inherited guilt). It did not say that we always only sin or that sinners are as bad as possible. And it did not deny free will—something Augustine went on to deny. Instead, the Council said only that all human beings except Jesus Christ stand in need of God's grace for both forgiveness and help to live righteous lives. There are no other exceptions.

This came to be the official, explicit orthodoxy of all major branches of Christianity even though Protestants tend to think Catholics lean too close to heresy whenever they talk of "merit" other than Jesus Christ's. Catholics, to say nothing of Protestants who follow Luther and Calvin, think the Eastern Orthodox churches lean too close to Pelagianism by denying inherited guilt. So orthodox Christians do not agree on the details of the human condition or salvation, but on the basics they agree—salvation itself is impossible without the supernatural grace of God; humans cannot save themselves or contribute to their salvation apart from special grace.

Semi-Pelagianism Seeks Middle Ground

After the controversy over Pelagius, Augustine went on to deny not only self-salvation but free will.[1] He affirmed predestination. For him, this was the only way to protect human inability due to sin and the absolute necessity of God's grace. He came to believe that free will itself opened the door to self-salvation. For those familiar with Calvinism, Augustine was a partial Calvinist before Calvin! (He didn't teach everything that Calvin did a millennium later.)

During Augustine's lifetime, a group of monks in Gaul (France) began to seek middle ground between Pelagianism and Augustine's strong view of God's sovereignty in salvation—unconditional predestination of some persons to salvation. The three main ones were Faustus of Riez, John Cassian, and Vincent of Leríns. Much later, their teaching came to be called "semi-Pelagianism," but many scholars believe it could just as well be called "semi-Augustinianism." They were well acquainted with Augustine's writings and teachings and embraced most them, but they were uncomfortable with his late emphasis on predestination and denial of free will. So they sought a compromise that would take the best of Pelagius's emphasis on human free will and Augustine's emphasis on the necessity of grace and combine them.

Again, as so often, what these "semis" believed and taught is not always easy to pin down, and the label *semi-Pelagianism* is not synonymous with everything they taught. For example, in the annals of Christian history and theology it *does not* mean belief in free will. Semi-Pelagianism has come to be used *only* for these compromising theologians' belief that human persons are not so damaged by original sin that they cannot, of themselves, without supernatural grace, initiate a good will toward God. That is, they taught that normally the initiative in salvation is on the human side. Cassian wrote that the first exercise of a good will toward God is the sinners' without supernatural prevenient grace. This came to be the rejected part of semi-Pelagianism, not these theologians' emphasis on free will that both the Eastern and Western churches accepted as orthodox. (Although it should be said that the Catholic Church permits belief in predestination, so long as it does not make God responsible for sin or take away human responsibility.)

In 529, a council of Western bishops met at Orange in Gaul to consider, among other things, whether semi-Pelagianism should be condemned as heresy. That it did. The synod (not an ecumenical council because bishops from the East were not present) rejected the belief that sinners are capable of initiating a saving relationship with God or cooperating with grace in any way that would lessen the necessity of grace or give saved persons room to boast. It also condemned any belief that God predestines anyone to evil (so, "double predestination"). It affirmed that sinners rely entirely on grace even to exercise a first movement of the will toward God. All Catholics and most Protestants agree with this and consider semi-Pelagianism "heterodox" if not heretical. (*Heterodoxy*, which means "outside of orthodoxy," is not quite as serious as heresy.)

While outright Pelagianism was virtually wiped out within all branches of Christianity by the Council of Ephesus, semi-Pelagianism has never been as thoroughly eliminated from Christian ranks. And what exactly *counts* as semi-Pelagianism is still debated to this day. (Here I am going by the common definition of it as that which was condemned and excluded by the Synod of Orange in 529.) Some very strict predestinarians, monergists, will claim that any Christian belief in free will in matters pertaining to salvation is semi-Pelagian, but that stretches the term too far. Most orthodox Catholics believe in free will, as do most orthodox Protestants. (For example, even though Luther did not believe in free will, his successor as leading theologian of the Lutherans in Europe, Philipp Melanchthon, did. And even though most Calvinists do not believe in free will, all Methodists and Anabaptists do.)

Modern Pelagianism and Semi-Pelagianism

Before turning to real examples of modern Pelagianism and semi-Pelagianism we will look briefly at a false "example." Many conservative Protestants in the Lutheran and Reformed (e.g., Presbyterian) traditions have long argued that Arminianism is Pelagian or (at best) semi-Pelagian. Arminianism is the belief, named after Jacob Arminius of Holland (d. 1609), that although salvation is by grace through faith alone, grace can be resisted and must be freely accepted. It is belief in freedom of the will among Protestants and is especially common in the Methodist tradition (including all denominations primarily inspired by it such as Pentecostalism). Although many people in Arminian churches may fall into Pelagianism or semi-Pelagianism, neither one was taught by Arminius or his more famous follower John Wesley.[2] Classical Arminian theology emphasizes prevenient grace and "freed will." That is, Arminianism believes that, apart from the prevenient grace of God, everyone's will would be so corrupted by inherited sin from Adam that it would be in a state of bondage to sin. God, however, frees the will of the person under the influence of God's word to make a decision to believe and receive salvation or reject the gospel and continue in a state of alienation from God.

Arminianism places emphasis on God's initiative in salvation and denies that sinners are capable, apart from special grace, of exercising a good will toward God. Therefore, it is neither Pelagian nor semi-Pelagian.

All one has to do to find modern Pelagianism and semi-Pelagianism is scratch the surface of American folk religion; both are rampant in it. Popular sayings such as "God helps those who help themselves" promote human effort in cooperation with God and human initiative in salvation. Television programs that include a religious theme usually fall into Pelagianism or semi-Pelagianism. A popular American television series that ran from 1994 to 2003 was called *Touched by an Angel.* The program featured a group of angels taking human form and trying to help depressed and down-and-out ordinary people. Sometimes the angels' message to the people verged on Pelagianism or at least semi-Pelagianism. In one scene, a dying man tells an angel that God could never forgive him. The angel tells him that all he needs to do is to climb up toward God and reach out and then God will reach back and take him the rest of the way. That is, of course, at least semi-Pelagianism.

But the writers of *Touched by an Angel* are no more to be blamed for falling into error about salvation than the majority of American Christians, including many seminary-trained pastors. Gospel songs and sermons often portray salvation that way—as if the Savior is standing at a distance "waiting" to enter a sinner's heart and all the sinner has to do is take a step toward him and "let him come in." Semi-Pelagianism, if not outright Pelagianism, is the default theology of most American Christians. Few sermons or popular Christian books or songs sung in churches teach the truth of prevenient grace and the absolute necessity of grace for any good that people do including the first exercise of a good will toward God.

One great American evangelist and theologian is often singled out for special blame for injecting semi-Pelagianism into American Christianity—Charles Finney (d. 1875). Finney was the most influential evangelist of the Second Great Awakening and was also a scholar who became president of Oberlin College. He certainly did not intend to teach Pelagianism or semi-Pelagianism, but some of his statements about salvation (e.g., in his *Lectures on Revivals of Religion* and *Systematic Theology*) certainly verge on at least the latter. He denied inherited depravity and the absolute necessity of prevenient grace (except as God's revealed will and universal call) and at least left the impression that sinners are capable of responding to the gospel with faith apart from supernatural enabling grace.

A later evangelist was Billy Sunday (d. 1935) who probably fell headlong into semi-Pelagianism if not outright Pelagianism, as did many American revivalists of the twentieth century. Sunday made revivals and conversions dependent on human effort—even bragging that he could save a soul for three dollars.

Very few, if any, Christian leaders in orthodox churches consciously embrace or promote Pelagianism. Many promote semi-Pelagianism without knowing it. But are there any modern or contemporary examples of outright

Pelagianism or semi-Pelagianism consciously embraced and promoted by people calling themselves Christians? That's a theological judgment call as no one, to the best of my knowledge, uses that terminology for their theologies of salvation. However, one reason orthodox Christians of all denominational affiliations have rejected Mormonism (the religious ethos and culture of the Church of Jesus Christ of Latter-day Saints and its offshoots) is strong suspicion that it rejects original sin and teaches sinners' unaided ability to convert to Christ. In other words, many conservative Catholics and Protestants believe that Mormon theology strongly implies a kind of humanism that makes grace unnecessary for the first exercise of the will toward God and in which good works contribute to salvation.

One finds serious disagreement about this among Mormons (who prefer to be called Latter-day Saints) themselves. One of the LDS Church's most influential theologians during the 1950s was Bruce R. McConkie (d. 1985). He was a member of the "Quorum of the Twelve Apostles"—the top council of the LDS Church. His book *Mormon Doctrine* (1958) inclines toward either Pelagianism or semi-Pelagianism by denying original sin and salvation by grace alone. According to him,

> One of the untrue doctrines found in modern Christendom is the concept that man can gain salvation . . . by grace alone and without obedience. This soul-destroying doctrine has the obvious effect of lessening the determination of an individual to conform to all the laws and ordinances of the gospel, such conformity being essential if the sought for reward is in reality to be gained.[3]

If that isn't Pelagianism or at least semi-Pelagianism it would be difficult to know what would be.

Another Mormon authority, also a member of the Quorum of the Twelve Apostles, was James Talmage (d. 1933). His book *A Study of the Articles of Faith* (1890) was republished by the LDS Church many times including in 1971 (forty-second edition). Talmage described the doctrine of salvation by grace alone through faith alone "a most pernicious doctrine"[4] and promoted salvation by faith and works. According to him, "Our condition in the world to come will be strictly a result of the life we lead in this probation [life on earth]."[5] The context makes clear that "the life we lead [here]" means faith and good works.[6] Talmage does not mention prevenient grace as necessary for faith or good works. The clear implication (and apparently many if not most Mormons have drawn it) is that sinners are fully capable of entering into salvation by their own effort.

That last statement is challenged, however, by a leading contemporary LDS theologian who teaches religion at Brigham Young University and has become a major ambassador of Mormonism to the wider Christian world. Robert Millet has published several books trying to explain Mormon doctrine to non-Mormons, especially evangelical Protestants, in a way that shows it to be closer to Christian orthodoxy than most people have supposed. Among them is *Grace Works* (2009) in which the author argues that Mormonism is a theology of grace even if many Mormons do not realize it. According to him, the Mormon doctrine of salvation only requires good works as evidence of grace active in a person's life. Good works do not force grace and salvation is not merited by good works. Millet stops short of endorsing "justification by faith alone," but his description of Mormon doctrine moves it away from Pelagianism if not from semi-Pelagianism.

Some branches and offshoots of the nineteenth-century Adventist movement have elevated good works over grace and faith as necessary for salvation. Many Christians once thought the Seventh-day Adventist Church did that, but that is no longer believed by informed Christians. (Which is not to say individual Seventh-day Adventists never fall into Pelagianism!) The Watchtower Bible and Tract Society (the denomination of Jehovah's Witnesses) is an offshoot of the Adventist movement that went in a very different direction from the Seventh-day Adventist Church (which is generally orthodox in its beliefs). Not only do Jehovah's Witnesses deny the deity of Christ and the Trinity, they also deny original sin and salvation by grace alone. Good works (e.g., "publishing"—going door-to-door selling Jehovah's Witness publications) are necessary for full salvation.

There are other, smaller offshoots of the Adventist movement that, like the Jehovah's Witnesses, deny the deity of Christ, the Trinity, and salvation by grace alone. In many cases, however, it is difficult to know exactly what the official teaching of many "smaller sects" is because they do not publish them for public consumption. The key question to ask is, "Does your church teach that grace is necessary for conversion to Christ and that full and final salvation is by grace alone through faith and not given as a reward for good works?" Of course, many "ordinary laypeople" in even orthodox Christian churches would have a hard time answering that; so examination of the church's doctrinal statement and gentle questioning of the pastor or other leader of the church is usually required to discover the answer.

Antidotes to Pelagianism and Semi-Pelagianism

The best antidotes to Pelagianism and semi-Pelagianism are the Bible, Christian tradition, reason, and experience. Of course, these have to be sensitively applied in preaching and teaching (including writing books, articles, and song lyrics). Bashing people with "orthodox doctrine" rarely helps—especially in our contemporary postmodern culture where everything is tolerated except intolerance. Words like *orthodoxy* and *tradition* turn many people off. On the other hand, in reaction to relativism and nondoctrinal religion, many people are seeking a more vibrant, robust, and "thick" description of Christian faith.

Scripture clearly teaches that *"there is no one who looks for God"* (Rom 3:11b). The doctrine of utter helplessness even to seek God on our own is deeply imbedded in the Bible's portrait of the natural person unaided by grace.

The Christian tradition also clearly holds to the doctrine of human inability to contribute to salvation by effort or good works without grace. Some readers may wonder about that. What about Catholic doctrine? Is it that salvation is by grace and good works? Not exactly. Rather, according to Catholic doctrine, salvation is by grace through faith and works of love, but both faith and works of love are considered grace-enabled. Truly meritorious good works, works that deserve praise, are products of grace as are all good things a person has or does. Protestants wince when Catholics talk about human "merit" in salvation because "merit" usually implies reward, which seems to take away from the gift nature of salvation. However, Catholic theology distinguishes between "condign merit" and "congruous merit." The former is merit that justly requires the reward; the latter is merit that does not match the reward and is, therefore, dependent on grace. In classical Catholic theology, even the meritorious good works of a Christian are dependent on gratuitous grace—God's undeserved gift.

Even Protestant reformers such as John Calvin believed that God rewards good works in heaven and that there will be unequal rewards dispensed there depending on human effort and sacrifice for God and others. Both Protestants and Catholics, however, believe that reconciliation with God that guarantees heaven is only through God's grace, even if good works cannot be separated entirely from "heavenly reward."

A person might wonder how reason enters into this matter. If God is really God, how can human achievement put God in our debt? It would seem incongruous to believe that God can be indebted to humans and especially sinful humans. Yet, Pelagianism does imply that. Also, why would Christ have died for everyone if it is possible to live a perfectly obedient life and never need grace? Reason working within a Christian framework of belief points away from Pelagianism and semi-Pelagianism.

Finally, experience militates against Pelagianism and semi-Pelagianism. Who can legitimately claim to be so good as to deserve God's favor? All stand in need of God's mercy and mercy is never owed to anyone. Every thoughtful human person knows he or she has fallen short of God's own righteousness and of his expectations of them. The law of God stands in judgment over all for "all have sinned and fall short of God's glory" (Rom 3:23).

The heresies of Pelagianism and semi-Pelagianism would never even occur to someone steeped in the basic Christian truth that everything good is a gift from God. "Every good gift, every perfect gift, comes from above. These gifts come down from the Father, the creator of heavenly lights, in whose character there is no change at all" (Jas 1:17). Scripture, tradition, reason, and experience point to the fundamental truth that nothing truly good is a product of human effort or achievement alone and that grace overshadows and surrounds and undergirds everything true, beautiful, and good.

Bringing It Home

1. What is your understanding of grace? What is the relationship between God's grace and human good works?

2. When we say things like, "God helps those who help themselves," how does that deny God's grace?

3. Grace is an undeserved gift from God. What other gifts does God give?

4. Share a time when you experienced the grace of God. How can Christians be channels of God's grace for others?

5. What does it mean when someone says, "There but for the grace of God go I"?

Chapter 8

Making God a Monster

Divine Determinism

A Different Kind of "Heresy"

So far we have been looking at *official* heresies of Christianity—beliefs rejected by ecumenical councils of the undivided church and by the major Protestant reformers of the sixteenth century and beyond. These have been doctrines that nearly all Christian leaders of all major branches of Christianity have labeled heresies. In these last three chapters we are going to look at beliefs common among Christians that are seriously wrong and destructive of the gospel but never condemned as heresies by ecumenical councils. Inevitably, then, a certain amount of individual, personal value judgment, and subjectivity comes into play in pronouncing them heresies.

I believe that, if approached about these beliefs, nearly all of the early Christian fathers and mothers, to say nothing of the apostles, would have been horrified and would have rejected them. They are, to say the least, extremely controversial among Christians and have been for a very long time—since they first appeared among Christians. Unfortunately, each one sounds reasonable and even appealing to some very devout followers of Jesus Christ. Each one is rising in popularity in the early part of the twenty-first century. Each one is causing significant concern and even turmoil in Christian circles, especially where *beliefs* are taken seriously as important to authentic Christianity.

In these three final cases, then, the word *heresy* shifts meaning somewhat. In these cases it is not "official" but unofficial, a matter of debate and controversy among authentic Christian folks but, in my judgment and others', nevertheless an appropriate epithet. That is to say, I could not affiliate with a church that promotes one or more of these beliefs because, although they contain a kernel of truth (nearly all heresies do), they distort the gospel out of recognition. In each case the "good news" becomes bad news. That's not always apparent at first, but with closer examination and reasonable interpretation, it becomes clear. Unfortunately, many Christians do not examine these beliefs; they simply swallow them whole because the persons teaching them seem so spiritual or the beliefs are popular and appear practical.

It never feels good to declare something fellow Christians believe "heresy." The immediate implication, not always correct, is that one is saying those who believe it are heretics. As mentioned and discussed in the first chapter, however, that is not necessarily so. A heretic is a person who knows what he is *teaching* (not merely *believing*) is contrary to the standard, confessional doctrinal beliefs of his faith community. People who merely believe a wrong teaching, a heresy, are not heretics. Even people who teach them are not necessarily heretics. They deserve to be called heretics when they know what they teach goes against the standard doctrine of their own faith community.

Let's look at that again. Salvation "by grace alone through faith alone" is heresy within a Roman Catholic context. A person who teaches it is only a heretic when he or she teaches it within a Roman Catholic context and knows it is "flat out" contrary to Catholic doctrine (i.e., the Canons and Decrees of the Council of Trent). A Protestant teaching it within a Protestant context is certainly *not* teaching heresy and cannot *be* a heretic because that is standard Protestant belief.

The decision by a faith community that a doctrine is heresy usually comes slowly. Someone has to start the ball rolling, so to speak, toward a consensus that it is contrary to the faith community's common, standard beliefs. That "rolling ball" process necessarily includes the risk of calling a popular belief within a faith community "heresy." But saying so does *not* necessarily include calling those who believe and teach it "heretics." They can't be heretics unless and until what they teach is somehow officially declared fundamentally wrong by the faith community. Then people who continue to teach it are rightly considered heretics insofar as they have been instructed.

Here, in these last chapters, I take the risk of declaring certain beliefs common among Christians "heresies." I am not, however, thereby calling those who believe them or even teach them "heretics." I am not talking about *people* but about *beliefs*. One of the tasks of theology is to critically examine beliefs labeled *Christian* to determine whether they deserve that appellation. The criteria for such determination are *revelation* (Jesus Christ, scripture), *tradition, reason*, and *experience*. This is what some have called the "Wesleyan Quadrilateral"—the four sources and norms of theological work. My claim about these final beliefs under consideration is that they constitute heresies, because they fundamentally contradict *revelation, tradition, reason*, and *experience*.

What Is *Divine Determinism?*

In the words of one very popular Christian pastor, teacher, author, and evangelist, absolutely everything that happens, without exception, was "planned, ordained, and governed" by God. That is standard Augustinian and Calvinist teaching. The early Christian bishop and church father Augustine taught that. The Protestant reformer John Calvin wholeheartedly agreed, as did his lesser-known predecessor in the Swiss reformation Ulrich Zwingli. Throughout Christian history, at least since Augustine, belief that God is the all-determining reality, that God designs, ordains, and governs whatever happens without exception, has been common and popular—especially among that branch of Protestantism known as "Reformed." Reformed Protestant Christianity has traditionally specialized in emphasizing God's sovereignty, God's providence over and predestination of all things. But that theme did not begin with the rise of Reformed Protestantism in Europe during the Reformation; it can be found here and there among Catholic Christians going back at least to Augustine in the fifth century.

For our purposes here, *divine determinism* means belief, whether explicit or implicit, that God determines all things according to a preconceived plan and by his omnipotent power, including sin and evil.

By all accounts Augustine of Hippo was the most influential church father and early theologian on Western (Latin) Christianity from the fifth century until at least the Reformation. He wrote numerous books and struggled against heresies such as Pelagianism and Donatism. His treatises on the Trinity and grace and his magnum opus *The City of God* are generally considered standard, foundational works of theology especially for Catholics and magisterial Protestants (e.g., Lutherans and Anglicans). But none of that means he is above criticism. Luther criticized Augustine, whom he greatly admired, for not understanding justification by grace through faith alone. The Anabaptists, the "radical reformers," broke with Augustine over many subjects but especially infant baptism as saving and the authority of the state over the church.

But perhaps no doctrines of Augustine's have been as controversial among both Catholics and Protestants as his teachings about God's sovereignty: meticulous providence and unconditional predestination. And it is doubtful that any Christian teacher or theologian before Augustine taught these doctrines as he did.

God's sovereignty is God's rule over the world and especially over history. Christian theologians have often distinguished between God's sovereignty *de jure* and *de facto*. The first, "de jure," is God's *right* to rule; the second, "de facto," is God's actual *control* of events. Augustine believed the distinction merely notional; for him God is *both* sovereign "de jure" *and* "de facto" at all times. Non-Augustinian theologians often argue that God is always sovereign *de jure* but not yet sovereign *de facto*. That is, God has the right to exercise meticulous control over all events, determining everything about them, but God chooses not to determine everything yet. That allows creatures such as human persons to resist God's perfect will, which is how sin and evil entered the world. If God is always already sovereign *de facto*, then the question naturally arises about God's authorship of sin and evil.

To recap briefly, then, some Christians, following Augustine's teaching, have believed that God exercises meticulous, detailed, "fine grained" sovereignty over everything—down to the most minute details of history and individuals' lives. Nothing, then, is out of God's will or control. Of course, there are variations of this belief; different Christian theologians have expressed it differently. Some Christians, on the other hand, have believed that God is sovereign by right and, because he is omnipotent, *could* control everything meticulously, but that God does not exercise such minute control. According to the first few, Augustine and those who follow him, human persons are not free to resist God's will; according to the second view, that of, for example John Wesley, human persons are free to resist God's will because God permits it. God is sovereign over his sovereignty; he limits his power to make room for creaturely decision-making power.

Here is how Augustine expressed his view of God's sovereignty, expressed with regard to human decisions and actions: "For the Almighty [God] sets in motion even in the innermost hearts of men the movement of their will, so that He does through their agency whatsoever He wishes to perform through them."[1] Augustine did not think this was occasional; it was for him the constant and unbroken method of God in bringing about his plan. In what sense, then, are people "free"? The North African church father explained that people are free whenever they do what they want to do, even if they could not have done otherwise. And there is a sense in which no one could really do otherwise than they do. God controls everything, including human decisions and actions, according to a predetermined plan and purpose.

Why did Augustine teach this strong doctrine of divine sovereignty? There are several reasons, but perhaps chief among them is his idea of God—that God's sovereign will and power cannot be frustrated, thwarted by creatures. It is part of God's very nature, Augustine believed, to be in control of creation. He could not conceive of God being limited in any way, even by his own self-limitation.

Of course, Augustine's belief and teaching about God's sovereignty raises to an intense pitch the issue of sin and evil: Is God the author of them? Augustine answered negatively: no, God is not the author of sin and evil. And yet, many have asked, how can that be if God controls everything including the "movement" of creatures' wills? Augustine simply denied that this makes God the author of sin and evil as that, too, would offend the dignity of God. So he left it as a paradox—an unresolved apparent contradiction. Sin and evil stem from creatures' rebellious wills, not from God's will, although God wills to permit them and they, too, cannot fall outside God's overall sovereignty.

What I have been discussing so far is Augustine's doctrine of God's *providence*—God's sovereignty in relation to history and individuals' lives. The twin doctrine of God's sovereignty is *predestination*—God's will in relation to individuals' ultimate destiny in either heaven or hell. Following his strong view of providence, Augustine also believed and taught that God chooses whom to save without reference to their own personal, "free" choices. Everyone since Adam inherits his fallen nature, even his guilt, and is incapable of not sinning. God freely and graciously chooses some individuals out of this "mass of damnation" to save. They are the "elect." Most people associate this idea of predestination with Calvin and Calvinism, but it goes back at least to Augustine, who laid it out in Calvin-like fashion in one of his last treatises entitled "On the Predestination of the Saints." There he affirmed that if someone is saved it is solely due to God's gracious election of him or her and not due to a free decision made by the person or his or her parents (e.g., in infant baptism). This election of individuals to salvation is unconditional; it does not depend on God's foreknowledge of their faith (as in alternative views of election). When asked why some are elect, Augustine answered that "the reason why one person is assisted by grace and another is not helped, must be referred to the secret judgments of God . . . the hidden determinations of God."[2]

Augustine stopped short of teaching "double predestination." He denied that God predetermines anyone to hell; he simply chooses some to save and leaves others to their deserved judgment and damnation for disobeying God. Many critics have asked, however, how this differs from "double predestination." Isn't choosing some unconditionally and leaving others the same as predestining everyone either to heaven or hell?

Whether Augustine's view of God's sovereignty deserves the appellation "divine determinism" is much debated by scholars, but it seems to me that it does. Clearly, for Augustine, God determines everything—not just with reference to its *outcome* (e.g., in bringing good from it) but also with reference to its *genesis*—its beginning. Everything without exception is rendered certain by God according to his plan and purpose and by his power.

Whence, then, evil? Augustine attempted to get God "off the hook," so to speak, as the author of sin and evil by denying that evil is a "thing." Evil, he argued, is nothing but the absence of the good. So God, the creator of all things, is not its creator. Nothing is. According to him, the only evil thing is an evil will. No substance or being is intrinsically evil. Evil is only the twist, the brokenness, the deviation from the good given to something by a creature's rebellious will. Still, given what Augustine said about God's sovereignty and creatures' free will, it seems logical to conclude that sin and evil are part of God's plan and rendered certain by him—even if he does not directly *cause* them. However, Augustine drew back from saying that; he wanted to protect God from the stain of sin and evil and attribute it solely to creatures.

Our conclusion is, then, that Augustine's doctrine of God's sovereignty *logically implies* divine determinism *even with regard to sin and evil* even if he did not affirm that God determines them. Colloquially expressed, "he never worked it out."

However, some Christians during Augustine's lifetime and shortly afterward were afraid that his influence would eventually bring it about that Christians would view God as the author of sin and evil. So, at a synod of Catholic bishops held in the (now French) city of Orange in 529, the Second Council of Orange, belief that God "predestines to evil" was condemned as heresy. That is why a later Catholic theologian named Gottschalk was persecuted by the church and empire—because he drew out the logic of Augustine's belief and taught that God is the author of sin and evil. (Whether and to what extent Gottschalk actually taught this is unclear because we only know about him from church records and he clearly was persecuted by the church because it believed he taught this—even after being instructed not to.)

Divine Determinism in Christian History

John Wycliffe is best known for his promotion of English Bible translation at a time (fourteenth century) when it was illegal. The Bible was to be read only in Latin in his time and place. However, Wycliffe was a forerunner of the Protestant Reformation that came to full flower in the sixteenth century with Luther, Zwingli, and Calvin. Wycliffe believed that salvation is by grace alone and through faith. He denied typical Catholic doctrines such as transubstantiation—that the bread and wine of the Lord's Supper become the actual body and blood of Christ. He promoted Bible study and gospel preaching in a way the later reformers did. For him, as for them, the Bible, not the pope or church councils, is the supreme authority over doctrine.

Wycliffe was a divine determinist. He followed Augustine's doctrine of God's sovereignty, going even further than the African church father in affirming God's meticulous control of all events including the damnation of the non-elect. He was a firm believer in "double predestination"—that doctrine of election most people associate with Calvin who came centuries after Wycliffe.

But perhaps the most stringent divine determinist in Christian history was Ulrich Zwingli, the reformer of the Swiss city of Zurich and contemporary of Luther. Zwingli held the strongest view of God's sovereignty imaginable. That it flat-out contradicted the dictates of the Second Council of Orange did not bother him; he and his city were at war with Catholics. (Zwingli died in a battle between Catholics and Protestants.) It's important to understand that Zwingli, the real "father" of Reformed Protestantism, was a nominalist and a voluntarist with regard to God's nature. That is, following the teachings of certain medieval "scholastic" philosophers, he believed that God has no eternal nature that controls, limits, or governs his will and power. In other words, there is no "law" to which God is bound, including one within his own nature. God is literally free to decree and cause anything he wills. Whatever God does is good *just because God wills it*. And everything that happens, without exception, happens because God wills it.

When discussing the fall of angels and humans and the salvation of some humans (the elect) Zwingli said, "God wrought both of these things."[3] Furthermore, according to the Swiss reformer, "The same deed which is done at the instigation and direction of God, brings honor to Him, while it is a crime and sin to man"[4] and "Although He impels men to some deed which is a wickedness unto the instrument that performs it, yet it is not such unto Himself. For his movements are free. . . . For He is not under the law."[5] Zwingli absolutely denied creaturely free will and attributed all things that happen to God—including sin and evil. Of course, he did not mean that God sins; he meant that God instigates sin for a greater good—his own "honor."

Zwingli came as close as any Christian theologian to making God the author of sin and evil. Speaking of David's adultery with Bathsheba, Zwingli said, "So far as concerns God as the author of it, it is no . . . sin to God."[6] Then, "The same deed which is done at the instigation of God, brings honor to Him, while it is a crime and sin to man. . . . And although he impels men to some deed which is a wickedness unto the instrument that performs it, yet it is not such unto Himself. . . . He instigates the robber . . . to kill even the innocent and those unprepared for death."[7] Zwingli's constant defense of God was that "He is not under the law"[8] and he meant that God is not under *any* law. He is absolutely free to do whatever he pleases.

The Swiss reformer of Zurich also affirmed double predestination without any sense of hesitation or embarrassment. According to him, "[The word] election is attributed to those only who are to be blessed, but those who are to be damned are not said to be elected, though the Divine Will makes disposition with regard to them also, but He rejects, expels and repudiates them, that they may become examples of His righteousness."[9] In the same context he denies free will, so even the "damned" sin and become condemned not by free choice but according to God's will.

Zwingli represents the clearest example of divine determinism in Christian history without qualification, subtlety, or complications. But what about his better-known Swiss counterpart in Geneva, John Calvin? Did Calvin teach divine determinism? He did, but with greater caution and more qualifications than Zwingli. Calvin, for example, strove *not* to make God the author of sin and evil while teaching God's supreme sovereignty over all things including the sin, evil, and eternal damnation of the nonelect who he called the "reprobate."

Calvin devoted great attention and space in his *Institutes of the Christian Religion* to God's sovereignty—including his providence and predestination. In sum, with regard to God's involvement in the evil deeds of the wicked, Calvin leaned as far away from saying that God is their author as possible while maintaining with Augustine and Zwingli that God rules over everything including sin and evil. According to Calvin, "Men can accomplish nothing except by God's secret command, . . . they cannot by deliberating accomplish anything except what he has already decreed with himself and determines by his secret direction."[10] The reformer of Geneva illustrated this principle by imagining a merchant who foolishly wanders away from his companions on a journey and is killed by robbers. According to Calvin, "His death was not only foreseen by God's eye, but also determined by his decree."[11] For "God by the bridle of his providence turns every event whatever way he wills."[12] Calvin clearly believed in meticulous providence.

How, then, did Calvin escape making God the author of sin and evil? He faced this question directly and responded by distinguishing between God's good purposes in everything he foreordains (and he foreordains everything!) and the creatures' evil purposes in acting wickedly. God wills everything for a good purpose; wicked people act out of evil intentions. "Through the bad wills of evil men God fulfills what he righteously wills."[13] But the question obviously arises about the source of wicked people's evil wills. In the final analysis, to get God "off the hook" and keep God unstained by any taint of evil Calvin fell back on God's permission—something he adamantly denied earlier. "In a wonderful and ineffable manner nothing is done without God's will, not even that which is against his will. For it would not be done if he did not permit it; yet he does not unwillingly permit it, but willingly."[14] In sum, according to Calvin, everything that happens, including sinful and evil deeds, are foreordained and rendered certain by God while God remains unstained by their wickedness because he does not force creatures but only permits them to sin. But God's permission of sin and evil is "willing permission." God is not the author of sin and evil because, although he foreordains and renders them certain, he does not directly cause them. Zwingli was clearer.

Most Reformed Christians follow Calvin's account of God's providence and predestination. (Calvin also taught "double predestination.") That is, they believe that God foreordains everything without exception and does not merely foreknow or foresee them. All things happen according to the plan and purpose of God; God does not merely bring good out of what is not good. God does not merely permit anything to happen but willingly permits sin and evil, which he has foreordained, because he plans to overcome them and through that reveal his greatness and glory. Many Reformed Christians simply admit there is a paradox here: God foreordains and renders certain everything, including sin and evil, but only permits sin and evil and is not their author.

Perhaps the most influential divine determinist in modern Christian history was Jonathan Edwards, the great Puritan preacher, philosopher, and theologian. Born in 1703 in Massachusetts, Edwards was contemporary with John Wesley, his English evangelical counterpart in the revival known as the Great Awakening. Edwards was Reformed; Wesley was Arminian (believing in free will and rejecting divine determinism and unconditional predestination—single or double). One of Edwards's most important treatises is *Dissertation Concerning the End [Purpose] for Which God Created the World*. There he tackled the thorny subject of why God created at all and the ultimate purpose of everything—from creation itself down to the tiniest speck of existence. Edwards's answer was that God himself, and most especially his "glory," is the ultimate purpose of everything. According to him, God "is the first, efficient cause and fountain, from whence all things originate. . . . He is the last, final cause for which they are made; the final term to which they all tend in their ultimate issue."[15] Most Christians would have no trouble agreeing with the second part of that thesis; trouble enters with the first part. For Edwards, God is the "efficient cause and fountain" from which all things come. Does this include sin, evil, innocent suffering, and hell? For Edwards it did. Even those exist only for the glory of God.

Cutting right to the chase, Edwards answered the problem of sin, evil, and hell in his sermon "The Justice of God in the Damnation of Sinners." With regard to sin, "God may permit sin, though the being of sin will certainly ensue on that permission; and so, by permission, he may dispose and order the event."[16] Then, immediately following that appeal to what Calvin called "willing permission" the Puritan preacher denied "chance" and "contingency." "If there were any such thing as chance, or mere contingence, and the very notion of it did not carry a gross absurdity . . . it would have been very unfit, that God should have left it to mere chance, whether man should fall or no."[17] In other words, the fall of humanity into sin and all its consequences were not merely possible; they were determined by God. In case anyone doubts it, Edwards soon wrote (a few paragraphs later) that God "determines everything by his own will."[18]

In "Freedom of the Will" Edwards sought to prove the very concept of free will incoherent and untenable, to say nothing of unbiblical. Even God, he argues, does not have free will in the sense of being really able to do otherwise than he does because he always does what is most fit and wise. Thus, everything is determined—even God's own actions and decisions. (Edwards does not actually say that about God, but it is necessarily implied by his vehement rejection of free will as logically incoherent.) According to Edwards, then, "The futurity of all future events is established by previous necessity."[19] That is the very definition of determinism; put God in as the ultimate determiner of all things and we have "divine determinism."

Edwards saw the problem of evil and responded to it. Like Calvin before him he appealed to God's permission of sin and evil, not actual causation, but made clear that such "permission" is willing and efficacious permission. An analogy would be a teacher who "permits" a student to fail by withholding the help the student would need to pass the course. Even sin and evil are part of God's great plan to glorify himself through creation as a whole and every part of it.

But the clearest evidence of Edwards's divine determinism, taken to an extreme, even beyond anything Zwingli considered, is his claim that God creates continuously; for him there is no autonomy of any part of creation and no continuation of creation apart from God's immediate creative power. In a statement that makes even many fans of Edwards shudder, the Puritan theologian said that God creates the whole world and everything in it *ex nihilo* at every moment.

Did Edwards make God the author of sin and evil? Here is the answer Edwards gave in "Freedom of the Will":

> If by "author of sin," is meant the permitter, or not hinderer of sin; and at
> the same time, a disposer of the state of events, in such a manner, for wise,
> holy and most excellent ends and purposes, that sin, if it be permitted and
> not hindered, will most certainly and infallibly follow: I say, if this be all

that is meant, by being the author of sin, I don't deny that God is the author of sin.[20]

In other words, Edwards said that while God does not coerce or force anyone to sin, he does design, ordain, and govern sin for a purpose. Sin is willed and rendered certain by God. At least he "bit the bullet" most Reformed Christians will not bite and admitted that God is the author of sin and evil in that sense.

Edwards also believed in double predestination. For him, the damned in hell are there because of their own perverse disobedience to God's revealed law *and* for the greater glory of God. Through hell God reveals his justice through wrath and makes the blessedness of the saved sweeter.

Contemporary Divine Determinism

In the last couple decades of the twentieth century and first two decades of the twenty-first, Reformed theology has been enjoying a renaissance—especially among college and university students. It is called the "Young, Restless, Reformed Movement." Several Reformed theologians and preachers have been instrumental in building and leading the movement. Among the most influential are R. C. Sproul, a Presbyterian, and John Piper, a Baptist. Both have written many books, spoken at large rallies and conferences, and appeared in films and podcasts. Both are charismatic personalities who can sway a crowd with their rhetoric.

Sproul considers himself a traditional Reformed and Calvinist theologian. He denies that he believes in "determinism," but he defines it as external compulsion or coercion—making someone act against their will. That is not how *determinism* is being used here or how it is defined in most dictionaries. The common definition of *determinism* is belief that everything that happens has a cause that renders it certain such that everything happens necessarily. When God is the ultimate cause that renders all things certain and necessary, "divine determinism" is in view.

One of Sproul's favorite sayings about God's sovereignty has to do with molecules. He tells audiences that if there is one maverick molecule in the universe not under God's control, then God is not God. He argues that anyone who does not agree that God controls everything ought to be a convinced atheist. For him, "predestination" does not have only to do with salvation (or not) but also with the cosmos and history. "It includes whatever comes to pass in time and space."[21] "The movement of every molecule, the actions of every plant, the falling of every star, the choices of every volitional creature, all of these are subject to [God's] sovereign will. No maverick molecules run loose in the universe, beyond the control of the Creator. If one such molecule existed, it could be the critical fly in the eternal ointment."[22]

What about sin and evil, then? Sproul attempts to get God off the hook as the author of sin and evil by distinguishing between God's "decretive will" and God's "permissive will," but he also affirms that whatever God permits, such as sin and evil, he decrees to permit. Like Edwards, then, Sproul believes and teaches that even sin and evil fall within the plan and purpose of God and are willed by God. Where does free will fit into this picture? According to Sproul, also following Edwards, there is no such thing as undetermined free will. *Free will* simply means doing what you want to do, not being forced to do something against your will. It does not mean being able to do otherwise than you do. He says, "There is a reason for every choice we make. In a narrow sense every choice we make is *determined*."[23] Ultimately, then, God, the all-determining reality, determines that people will sin, but somehow without causing them to sin. It seems fair to say that for Sproul, as for Augustine, Zwingli, and Edwards (if not for Calvin, too!), sin and evil are rendered certain by God for a greater good—the full revelation of God's glory.

It's important to say here that Sproul does not *intend* to make God the author of sin and evil. He probably draws back from even Edwards's admission that, in some highly qualified sense, God is the author of sin and evil. However, the logic of his doctrine of God's absolute, all-encompassing sovereignty leads inexorably in that direction. One cannot be blamed for calling his view a version of divine determinism even if he does not like that language.

John Piper is virtually unknown to most Christians over forty, but most evangelical Christians between eighteen and forty have probably read one of his books, watched one of his podcasts, perused his website, and perhaps even attended a conference where he spoke. Each year he is the premier speaker at a huge Christian youth event called "Passion." In the first few years of the second decade of the twenty-first century it attracts around fifty thousand Christian young people mostly under age twenty-six. It is no stretch to assume that hundreds of thousands of passionate Christian young people have come under his influence.

Piper makes no secret of his belief in what I am here calling divine determinism. Edwards is his inspiration, his muse, and he also makes no secret of that. Typical of his view of God's sovereignty in providence is his response to the 2001 terrorist attacks on New York and Washington, DC. On September 17, 2001, just days after the attacks, he posted a brief essay on his website entitled "Why I Do Not Say, 'God Did Not Cause the Calamity, but He Can Use It for Good.'" That's a complicated title for a very simple and straightforward essay. His foil is the common belief that "God, by his very nature, cannot or would not act to bring about such a calamity." His response: "This view of God is what contradicts the Bible and undercuts hope." He declared, "How God governs all events in the universe without sinning, and without removing responsibility from man, and with compassionate outcomes is mysterious indeed!" Then, "But that is what the Bible teaches. God 'works all things after the counsel of his will.'"[24]

Piper is bold in proclaiming the absolute sovereignty of God to the point of preaching that even if a "dirty bomb" fell on a city it would be from God. Whenever a disaster or calamity happens, including one that involves sin and innocent suffering, Piper boldly proclaims that it is "from God." He does not mean that God directly caused the perpetrators to sin—especially not against their own perverse wills. However, even their perverse wills are under the control of God's sovereignty. Nowhere does Piper say that God is the author of sin and evil, but it seems fair to assume that he agrees with Edwards.

Both Sproul and Piper believe, like Zwingli, Calvin, and Edwards, in double predestination. God foreordains which individuals will be saved and which will be damned. All deserve damnation (even though God foreordained and rendered certain the fall and all its consequences including human sinfulness) so God is merciful by showing some people mercy and saving them without any help from their own wills. All these Reformed theologians believe in unconditional election and irresistible grace.

Only a few Christian theologians are bold enough to draw out the logical conclusion from the Reformed theologians mentioned here: that God is the author of sin and evil. One notable one is R. C. Sproul Jr., son of the theologian mentioned before. In his 1999 book *Almighty over All,* the younger Sproul seems to break from his father and declares that God is the creator of sin and evil. How is God, then, not a sinner himself? Sproul Jr. follows Zwingli in explaining that God, being God, is above all law and whatever he does is automatically good just because he does it. That is nominalism and voluntarism as explained before. Many Reformed theologians would reject Sproul Jr.'s account of God's providence, preferring paradox instead: God designs, plans and governs sin and evil but is not their creator or author.

Why Divine Determinism Is Heresy (and What Should Be Done about It)

In my opinion, and many other Christians' opinions, making God the author of sin and evil is heresy. Most Reformed, Calvinist Christians do not fall into that. They are careful to keep a distance between God and evil. There is a difference between, for example, Sproul Sr.'s view and Sproul Jr.'s view. How great a difference is debatable, because it seems the son's view is simply the "good and necessary consequence" of the father's view. However, it's important not to attribute conclusions to people they expressly deny believing.

Most Christians throughout history have drawn a line between simple, garden-variety divine determinism and teaching that God is the author of sin and evil with the latter counting as heresy and the former not. For many Christians, including some Reformed ones, Sproul Jr. stepped over a line into heresy *at that one point*. That does not make him a heretic; that would depend on his ecclesial context—his community of faith and its doctrinal standards. However, one has to wonder what exactly the difference is—between ordinary divine determinism and declaring God the author (or creator) of sin and evil. If God being the author and creator of sin and evil is the good and necessary consequence of divine determinism, then doesn't that shadow fall over divine determinism itself?

One person who thought so, at least some of the time, was Methodist evangelist-founder John Wesley, who viciously attacked divine determinism in an essay entitled "Predestination Calmly Considered." There Wesley took on one particular aspect of divine determinism—the doctrine of "reprobation": that God alone decides who will be damned to hell. This, he argues, is the natural consequence of unconditional election—that God chooses to save some without any regard to their free decision to repent and believe and "pass over" others, leaving them to their "deserved damnation." "Single predestination" logically requires "double predestination" and thus the doctrine of reprobation. Of course, Wesley knew full well that if this doctrine could be proven wrong, the whole of divine determinism would fall with it.

Wesley appealed to the nature of God as love and to the goodness of God to disprove reprobation and thus God's foreordaining of sin and evil. Referring to the person God "passes over" according to divine determinism, Wesley asked, "Now, I beseech you to consider calmly, how is God good or loving to this man? Is not this such love as makes your blood run cold? As causes the ears of him that heareth to tingle? . . . Can you think, that the loving, the merciful God, ever dealt thus with any soul which he hath made? But you must believe this [viz., that he was made by God for damnation], if you believe unconditional election."[25] One could substitute "divine determinism" for "unconditional election" and Wesley's point would work against that broader viewpoint of which unconditional election is only a part.

The God of divine determinism *must be* the author of sin and evil, as Edwards admitted (with whatever qualifications). The only guard against it is sheer denial. It would seem, then, that all forms of divine determinism are on the precipice of heresy even if only calling God the author of sin and evil is outright heresy. Is it? Well, that's for churches and individuals to decide. I think it is. Many others think so, too. The Second Council of Orange of 529 certainly thought so!

What should be done about divine determinism? Again, that's up to individual denominations, congregations, and individuals. I, for one, could not attend a church (except to visit) that believed in or taught divine determinism because it undermines the good character of God as revealed in Jesus Christ. Why would Jesus have wept over Jerusalem for rejecting him and the prophets if God, including Jesus himself, had predetermined it for a greater good? What did Jesus mean by declaring God alone to be "good"? What does "good" mean if it includes authorship of sin and evil or even simply designing, ordaining, and governing (rendering certain) them? In what sense is God good if hell and all its occupants are part of God's design—God's will and decree?

Christian congregations and denominations ought to root out divine determinism, especially the view that God is the author of sin and evil, and perhaps also the view that God designed, ordained, and governs them.

Bringing It Home

1. The word *sin* has different meanings in the Bible. Consult a Bible dictionary and discuss the various meanings. Then use a

concordance to find the places in the Bible where the word is used. Do you believe that God is the author of sin?

2. Throughout church history, people have tried to understand why bad things happen, especially to good people. Does attributing evil and sin to God help settle the matter for you?

3. If God is love and God's love is steadfast, loving kindness, how can God also cause, allow, or permit evil? Do you see a difference between "causing" and "allowing" evil?

4. How does "double predestination" square with God's grace? Is anyone ever beyond the grace or help of God?

Chapter 9

Reducing God to Manageable Size

Moralistic Therapeutic Deism

The Problem of "Folk Religion"

Not everything that deserves the epithet *heresy* appears in the form of intellectual or scholarly theology. Sometimes, as in the ideas considered here and in the final chapter, heresy rears its ugly head in the form of what some sociologists of religion call "folk religion." According to sociologist of religion Robert Ellwood, all religions go through cycles, the last stage of which is folk religion—the loss of tradition and intellectual engagement with culture and the devolving of the religion into individualistic, privatized spirituality that thrives on clichés, popular beliefs, feelings, and experiences. Perhaps this is what sociologists Christian Smith and Melinda Denton refer to in their startling conclusion, based on their massive 2003–2005 National Study of Youth and Religion that

> we have come with some confidence to believe that a significant part of Christianity in the United States is actually only tenuously Christian in any sense that is seriously connected to the actual historical Christian tradition. . . . It is not so much that U. S. Christianity is being secularized. Rather, more subtly, Christianity is either degenerating into a pathetic version of

itself or . . . Christianity is actively being colonized and displaced by quite a different religious faith.[1]

Practical theologian Kenda Creasy Dean borrows John Wesley's phrase "almost Christian" to describe this condition. Many observers and commentators on contemporary American Christianity agree with her, Smith, and Denton's thesis that vast swatches of American Christianity are falling into a folk religion they call "Moralistic Therapeutic Deism" (MTD) that is at best a dim reflection and faint echo of real, robust, biblical, historical Christianity. And the trouble is that the people adopting MTD, mostly young people but not exclusively, think it's Christianity.

This chapter will focus on Deism in general and its living expressions in contemporary Christianity. MTD is but one version of it and some Deists warn MTD is not authentically Deist. The word *Deism* has taken on a much broader semantic range than it had in the eighteenth century when Thomas Jefferson embodied it. The thesis of this chapter is twofold: (1) Deism is a heresy, and (2) it is still very much alive and well and an attractive option for many Christians. The next and final chapter will focus on a flourishing heresy in American folk Christianity almost opposite of Deism—the "Gospel of Health and Wealth," rooted in nineteenth-century New Thought.

Both contemporary Deism, especially MTD, and the Gospel of Health and Wealth (GHW) have become American folk religions widely confused with Christianity. Many devout Christians adopt one or the other as their primary theological belief system without any awareness that they are really alternatives to biblical, orthodox Christianity. They are heresies only in the informal sense that they stand in such stark contrast to the gospel of Jesus Christ and historic, orthodox Christianity that they are hardly recognizable as Christian. Neither one existed in ancient Christianity; both are influenced by modern cultural, philosophical, and religious impulses and movements that have crept into Christian circles almost unnoticed. However, anyone knowledgeable about ancient or Reformation Christianity knows how strongly all the major leaders of past ecumenical Christianity would have reacted against them, had they known of them.

In order to understand MTD and GHW, it's important to know about "folk religion." Folk religion is to religion what folk medicine is to the science of medicine and what folk psychology is to the science of psychology. Folk medicine is, of course, popular beliefs about the sources of illnesses and wellness that may have some scientific support but, overall and in general, have no rational basis. That's not to say its "cures" never work! But it is to say that, insofar as it shuns modern medicine in favor of traditional folk remedies, it is more likely to do harm than good. An obvious example is the old saying "An apple a day keeps the doctor away." Nobody denies that apples are good, but modern science proves that the saying is not reliable. Apples are not a panacea as implied. Folk psychology says things like "Happiness is a choice." While there may be a seed of truth in that, anyone suffering from depression caused by an imbalance of brain chemistry knows it's not the whole truth and can be very damaging when said to him or her.

Folk religion replaces tradition, orthodoxy, scholarship, inquiry, biblical hermeneutics, and theology with beliefs based on comfort and spiritual excitement or satisfaction. It thrives on clichés that fit on bumper stickers such as "Don't worry; God is in control" and "In case of rapture this car will be driverless." It specializes in unverifiable "evangelegends" that only gullible people would believe such as that scientists drilling holes in the earth's crust broke through to hell and heard the screams of the damned. It replaces biblical and theological teachings about life after death with "testimonies" of near death or death experiences in books and movies. Folk religion is resistant to examination and critical thinking and tends to be relativistic—resting on results and especially good feelings.

Folk religion is to historic religion what astrology is to astronomy. It values blind faith, unexamined belief, religion that "works" in terms of helping people cope with the difficulties of life apart from tradition and community.

Not all folk religion is totally wrong or heretical, but it's a fertile seedbed in which heresy can grow and flourish. And folk religion divorces religion from public life and reduces it to a coping mechanism for individuals caught in the complexities of life. When a great world religion like Christianity is reduced to a folk religion it loses its ability to influence public, communal life together.

Moralistic Therapeutic Deism

According to Smith, Denton, Dean, and numerous other observers of contemporary American religious youth culture, something called Moralistic Therapeutic Deism is the preferred alternative to historical religious traditions including classical Christianity. Its core theme is "divinely underwritten personal happiness and inter-personal niceness."[2] MTD, they say, "is supplanting Christianity as the dominant religion in the United States."[3] If this is true, and many astute observers of American religious life agree that it is, it's startling and worthy of concern and pushback by pastors and Christian lay leaders.

So what is MTD? Various descriptions exist, but as Smith and Denton are its "discoverers," I'll follow their description (as does Dean). MTD has five "guiding beliefs":

(1) A god exists who created and orders the world and watches over life on earth. (2) God wants people to be good, nice, and fair to each other, as taught in the Bible and by most world religions. (3) The central goal of life is to be happy and to feel good about oneself. (4) God is not involved in my life except when I need God to resolve a problem. And (5) Good people go to heaven when they die.[4]

This is, admittedly, a "bare bones," skeletal outline of "mere MTD." Several points may be added. For example, most people who adopt MTD believe God punishes people who are not nice and good but forgives everyone who has good intentions and is sorry for their mistakes. Most MTD believers work Jesus into their MTD as the revelation of God's expectations, goodness, and love.

I think we have to distinguish between two types of MTD in contemporary religion. First is a non-Christian version that does not explicitly include Jesus Christ as anyone other than the founder of the Christian religion and perhaps a religious prophet. Second is a Christian version found especially among young people (now getting older and having families) raised in all kinds of Christian churches. This version is explicitly Christian *in the sense* of including Jesus Christ as the perfect revelation of God's will and forgiving love and as a friend who is always "there" to bring comfort and assurance. But the two versions overlap a great deal; in both, for example, God does not directly intervene or become involved in individual, personal life except when the person has a problem that only God can solve. And then God's role is mainly to give guidance, strength, and comfort.

MTD is supported by and expressed in many popular religious-themed songs. Bett Midler's extremely popular 1990 version of the song "From a Distance [God Is Watching Us]" expressed and reinforced a deistic view of

God for many people. The popular country gospel song "It's Me Again, Lord" by devout Christian songwriter Dottie Rambo seems to support the idea that God is just "there" for us when we have a problem we can't solve by ourselves.

The exact origins of MTD are difficult to trace and pin down. The main ingredient in it, however, seems to be Deism—an unorganized religion developed and embraced by religious "free thinkers" of the Enlightenment in Germany, France, and Great Britain especially in the eighteenth century. So to that I now turn.

Deism as a Historical Movement

Deism is the term usually used for a philosophical-religious belief system that arose without any organizational help in response to the Enlightenment in Europe. The Enlightenment was the cultural revolution launched by European intellectuals revolting against the authority of tradition and seeking new paths for knowledge through reason alone. It was given strong impetus by the wars of religion on the heels of the Reformation. During the first half of the seventeenth century, Protestants and Catholics slaughtered each other throughout much of Europe. Many intellectually minded elites of Europe sought a new foundation for religion and politics in universal reason. The beginnings of modern science were showing the way forward—knowledge of the universe based on observation and logic apart from revelation, tradition, and faith.

One of the first people to attempt to imitate science in religion was Lord Herbert of Cherbury, who died in 1648—the year in which the Thirty Years' War ended in Germany and the English Civil War between the Puritans and King Charles I was in full heat. During his lifetime Lord Herbert sought and believed he found a "religion of reason" that depended on no supernatural revelation from God or on church authority. Many commentators believe that what drove him to invent what later came to be known as Deism was his desire to bring peace to Great Britain and Europe by replacing "sectarian religion" with a minimal religion with which every reasonable person could agree.

Lord Herbert posited that all religion could be summed up in five "common notions": (1) that there is a supreme Deity; (2) that this Deity ought to be worshipped; (3) that virtue combined with piety is the chief part of divine worship; (4) that men should repent of their sins and turn from them; (5) that reward and punishment follow from the goodness and justice of God, both in this life and after it. The similarities between this account of religion and MTD are obvious. For both, God is good and cares about us but is un-involved in human life—except that according to Lord Herbert God metes out punishments and rewards and for MTD God is our "problem solver" (without clear definition or description of what that means).

There was no great rally to Lord Herbert's minimalist religion of reason, but it planted a seed that would flower into a movement in the next century. Between 1648 and the dawn of the eighteenth century, when Deism became a movement, the Enlightenment was born and began to change everything in European culture and eventually the whole world. In a phrase, it was the "Age of Reason," with new emphasis on knowledge through evidence and logic alone, putting aside revelation, tradition, and faith. Of course, many people clung to revelation, tradition, and faith, but as never before cultural elites, the movers and shakers of culture, turned their backs on traditional authorities and sought new answers for perennial questions in reason alone. One obvious example was the death of government by "divine right of kings" and the birth of "social contract theory" of government. The latter was and is the "natural law" approach to who should govern and how. The people give certain indi-viduals among them the right to rule and the people have the right to take it away. This was revolutionary thinking in politics.

One way to understand the Enlightenment, including the scientific revolution, is to think of the rational search for the natural laws governing everything. Isaac Newton discovered gravity and other natural laws of phys-ics. Enlightenment people began searching for natural laws that explain all phenomena. Eventually religion was subjected to such natural, rational expla-nation. Deism was the eighteenth-century movement in religion, involving some Christians and some non-Christians, called "natural religion." The idea, similar to Lord Herbert's much earlier, was to establish a religion based solely on natural reason without any appeal to anything supernatural and without granting special authority to traditional religious offices, doctrines, or books.

The first major publication in the movement was John Toland's 1696 book *Christianity Not Mysterious,* the subtitle of which was, "Showing that there is nothing in the gospel contrary to reason nor above it and that no Christian doctrine can be properly called a mystery." Although it was pub-lished in the late seventeenth century, it is really an eighteenth-century book in spirit. Toland was cautious; he did not openly deny miracles or the supernatural or any doctrine of the Christian faith protected by British blasphemy laws. (It was a criminal offense in Great Britain in 1696 to deny a standard doctrine of English orthodoxy, the teachings of the Church of England.) However, he argued that even divine revelation must be judged by reason and that any doctrine that was ultimately and finally mysterious, not capable of rational explanation, could not be essential to true religion—including Christianity.

Conservative Christian readers understood the trajectory Toland was on and where his teaching would lead—to the dissolution of Christian orthodoxy. He only openly attacked Catholic doctrines like "transubstantiation" (belief that in the Catholic mass the bread and wine actually become the body and blood of Christ)—safe targets in Anglican England. However, he trusted his readers to extrapolate his arguments against them to "mysterious" doctrines such as the Trinity and the incarnation. It is highly likely that he did not believe in those, either. Most readers understood that Toland was implying that true religion includes nothing supernatural.

His book was publicly burned by the city's hangman in Dublin, the capital of Toland's Irish homeland (which was then part of the United Kingdom of Great Britain and Ireland). Members of the Irish parliament called for him to be burned at the stake. England was more tolerant and allowed him to live and write, but he had great difficulty finding any university that would allow him to teach there.

Toland's book is usually considered the clarion announcement of the new religion of pure reason to come. One of the myths about Deism taught in most high schools and colleges is that Deism's god is distant, remote, and uninvolved in earth's matters. The god of Deism is often described as an "absentee landlord" of the world or as a clockmaker of nature who created it and its laws but set it down and never interferes. There's truth to the idea of non-interference, but Toland actually considered himself a "pantheist"—someone who believes in an identity of nature and god. His god was not remote, distant, or uninvolved, but neither was he or it in the habit of ever interfering in how the world goes. It "goes" according to natural laws that cannot be broken even by god. Toland did not say that (to say it would have gotten him arrested), but most scholars believe that was his idea of God and the world. So popular teaching about Deism's god is often based on a stereotype based on a partial misconception.

Another British scholar went further than Toland; in 1730, Matthew Tindal wrote *Christianity as Old as the Creation; or, the Gospel a Republication of the Religion of Nature*. Some have dubbed it the real "Bible" of Deism, but Tindal seemed to draw out the implications of Toland's earlier work. Both Toland and Tindal redefined "Christianity." For Tindal, Christianity is *not* a set of supernaturally revealed truths surrounding miracles and it does *not* include any suprarational beliefs. It is, as the title of his book implies, simply the universal beliefs of all rational people everywhere—about God, the soul, right and wrong, life after death. It is what is common to all great world religions, so Tindal believed. Basically, Tindal reduced Christianity to what might be called *ethical monotheism*—belief in a personal God who created and governs the world and who is best worshipped by living a good life according to natural law ethics—intuitive knowledge of right and wrong.

There were other Deists than Tindal and Toland. One French Deist, who preferred to call his belief system "Theism," was the free-thinker, playwright, and essayist Voltaire who loved to ridicule the Catholic Church and everything associated with orthodox Christianity. He believed in God but did not think it was possible to know very much about him; for him, true worship is simply living an ethical life according to reason. Voltaire (d. 1778) even created his own church, which had only one congregation and no priest or pastor. He claimed to "adore God," but his god was not the God of traditional, orthodox Christianity but the architect of the world, its supreme moral governor, and the rewarder of those who live according to reason.

Perhaps the best known of all Deists was Thomas Jefferson, third president of the United States. So impressed was he with Toland, Tindal, Voltaire, and other "free thinkers" that he created his own version of the Bible known popularly as "Jefferson's Bible." The title he gave it was *The Life and Morals of Jesus of Nazareth*. It was not published until 1820—long after he left the White House. Jefferson cut out of the New Testament (and his "Bible" consisted only of parts of that) everything he considered contrary to reason and natural morality and included only what he considered the timeless and reasonable teachings of Jesus. Everything miraculous and supernatural was excised. Jefferson did not join the then relatively new Unitarian Church as many Deists did; he remained nominally a member of the Episcopal Church. But he described himself to a friend as "a sect by myself." Most scholars consider Jefferson a Deist who greatly admired Jesus and considered himself a Christian even if the only one of his kind.

As with all great movements, Deism eventually "went to seed" as it was vulgarized by popularizers such as Thomas Paine and Ethan Allen, the heroic revolutionary leader of the "Green Mountain Boys." Both became popular writers of virulent tracts attacking Christianity and promoting their own versions of Deism. Theirs is the version of Deism often taught and criticized in orthodox Christian churches. President Theodore Roosevelt referred to Paine as "that filthy little atheist."[5] Also like most movements, Deism died out but filtered into the fabric of American culture. Elements of it pop up in unpredictable and unexpected places.

Deism's Subtle Influences on American Culture

If you google the word *Deism* numerous websites promoting it will appear. There is, however, no large organized religion or denomination of Deists. Instead, elements of Deism can be found scattered throughout American culture. It has become a permanent feature of American folk religion. I once read a newspaper profile of a science professor at a Christian university. He called himself a Methodist but named his own, personal religion as Deism. Many intellectuals adopt Deism, adapting it to their own spiritual needs, as their personal religion. Like the above-mentioned Christian university scientist, they may belong to a church that is not officially deistic. What attracts them to Deism, it seems, is their belief in God combined with belief in a universe ruled by iron-clad natural laws. They do not see any way to combine modern science with belief in miracles. What they have done, of course, as many Christian philosophers have pointed out, is confused science with naturalism—belief that nature is all there is and that nature is a closed network of causes and effects describable exhaustively mathematically. And yet, unlike "pure naturalists," they are unwilling to give up believing in God. They are not atheists. They are, to use Søren Kierkegaard's language, "almost Christian." Of course, most of them think of themselves as wholly Christian because they believe Jesus is the most perfect revelation of God's will for human behavior.

Another manifestation of Deism in culture is what some sociologists have labeled "civil religion"—belief in God as the guarantor of the rights of individuals and the rules that govern American constitutional polity. For many

Americans, "In God We Trust" is simply an expression of Deism. For them God established the truths upon which American law is based. For example, the "Declaration of Independence," written mainly by Jefferson, says that all people are endowed by God with "inalienable rights." Jefferson was combining Deism with social contract theory to justify the American revolt against Great Britain. But civil religion goes no further; it stops at the threshold of Jesus and Christian orthodoxy and worship. The "god" of civil religion may be overlaid in individuals' minds with Christian symbolism and even doctrines, but in public spaces that deity is simply "the Almighty," "Providence," and/or "the Creator." He or it is an "unbaptized god," stripped and shorn of "sectarian" identity.

Finally, Deism appears in popular religion whenever people believe in a creator and moral governor of the universe who is uninvolved in day-to-day life but still somehow cares enough to help (e.g., with strength to endure troubles), punishes the truly wicked (e.g., Hitler), and forgives all who are sorry for their sins. Few who think of God this way would call their religion Deism; most consider themselves Christians. But their god is quite far removed from the passionate, intimately involved, intervening, relational God of the Bible who died on the cross, rose from the dead, and even sometimes raises the dead (and will eventually raise all the dead!).

The results of Smith and Denton's National Study of Youth and Religion came as a shock to many Christian leaders who assumed that American youth, especially those raised in church, were mainly Christian, even if sometimes confused about their Christianity. Kenda Creasy Dean, a widely respected scholar of youth culture and professor at Princeton Theological Seminary, dropped a bombshell on American Christianity with her book *Almost Christian*, which interpreted the findings of the National Study. For her, MTD is the natural result of "two and a half centuries of [churches] shacking up with 'the American dream.'"[6] Her challenging conclusion is that

> Churches have perfected a dicey codependence between consumer-driven therapeutic individualism and religious pragmatism. These theological proxies gnaw, termite-like, at our identity as the Body of Christ, eroding our ability to recognize that Jesus's life of self-giving love directly challenges the American gospel of self-fulfillment and self-actualization. Young people in contemporary culture prosper by following the latter. Yet Christian identity, and the "crown of rejoicing" that Wesley believed accompanied

147

consequential faith born out of a desire to love God and neighbor, requires the former.[7]

Some will dismiss Dean's conclusions as "Chicken Little" despair and say the sky is not falling. Even if her warning is only partially true, however, it deserves serious consideration. Is American Christianity accommodated to a culture that has little or nothing to do with the gospel and biblical, historic, classical Christianity? Has it largely morphed into a pale reflection of that? If so, is Deism its name?

Why Deism Is Heresy

Virtually all Christian leaders of the eighteenth century recognized Toland's and Tindal's Deism as heresy. Why? What was wrong with it? Every culture adapts Christianity to its own context. What made Deism deserving of the epithet *heresy*?

First of all, if it's heresy it's a strange kind of heresy, because it doesn't have a clear and distinct denial of Christian orthodoxy that aims at a particular doctrine of the faith. Rather, from a perspective rooted within orthodox Christianity of any denominational tradition, Deism appears to be really an alternative religion entirely. Would we call Buddhism a heresy? The language is problematic. However, the movers and shakers of Deism *claimed* it was Christianity. And for many later Deists, including contemporary ones, it *is* their *version* of Christianity. They see no incompatibility between it and the gospel. They hold fast to Jesus—as the human "face of God." In other words, for them Jesus was just a man who lived a perfect life and thereby revealed God's moral expectations for the rest of us.

Second, if it's heresy it's a difficult one to pin down, because it has become so much a part of the warp and woof of American religious culture. It rarely appears in any "pure" form; it appears mainly in certain attitudes, dispositions, and "fall-back beliefs" about God and salvation.

I would call anyone *primarily* a Deist who believes: (1) that God exists as the creator and moral governor of the universe but is uninvolved in daily life and never intervenes supernaturally in the courses of nature and history, and (2) religion is primarily, if not exclusively, about morality—living a "good life" of being nice to others and true to oneself. What's wrong with this religion? Why is it heresy?

It's heresy because it is "another gospel" than the one we find in the New Testament. The New Testament gospel, understood this way by all branches of historic, orthodox Christianity, is *not* that we achieve salvation by living a good moral life but *that* we are sinners who can only be saved by God's grace and that God has reached across the gulf between him and us caused by our sin to bring us salvation through Jesus Christ's death on the cross and his resurrection. In other words, according to Jesus and the apostles who wrote the New Testament, the church fathers and Protestant reformers, the great evangelists and teachers of all denominations in the past, and faithful theologians of the present, true religion is about *sin* and *grace*, not *being good*. In the words of a popular Christian song of the 1980s recorded by Amy Grant, "being good" is not possible in our own strength, so we have to "leave it to the Lord."[8]

John the Baptist and Jesus called for repentance, not better ethics. Jesus condemned the Pharisees and others who thought they achieved God's favor by keeping rules. He called people to believe and depend on him. Paul the apostle struggled mightily against Jews and Christians who wanted true religion to be a matter of rule keeping, and he emphasized repentance, being made new by the power of the Holy Spirit, and letting Christ live in them by faith defined as trust in the cross as God's action for our salvation.

In 2008, Christian scholar and popular teacher of authentic Christianity Mark Galli published a book that serves as a corrective to the image of Christ found in much American folk religion, including MTD. Galli, editor of *Christianity Today* magazine, wrote *Jesus Mean and Wild: The Unexpected Love of an Untamable God.*[9] Eugene Peterson, creator of the popular *The Message* paraphrase of the Bible, wrote the book's Foreword. According to the book, and this is faithful to the picture of Jesus we see in the Gospels, Jesus was not "meek and mild" and God is not "tame." Rather, Jesus demands trust in him above all others, reliance on his mercy, and even fear of his judgment. God is loving but not indulgent and calls his people to self-sacrifice, not self-actualization through being true to self and merely being nice.

Deism, including MTD, is heresy because it totally distorts the biblical and orthodox picture of God, our selves, and salvation. Although the gospel comforts the afflicted, giving hope and meaning in the midst of suffering, it is not about feeling good about yourself (the "therapeutic" part of MTD) or merely being nice or a God with high moral expectations who guarantees us success in life (salvation) if we obey his rules. The gospel is about entering into the kingdom of God at great risk to self in total trust in Jesus Christ as Savior and Lord of all.

Deism is heresy because it denies miracles. Of course, not everyone who is under the influence of MTD denies all miracles, but Deism leads away from belief in miracles, from a God who intervenes, toward a god who is "watching us from a distance." The one event in human history that (1) is essential to Christianity, and (2) cannot be anything other than a miracle (if it happened) is the resurrection of Jesus Christ. The Apostle Paul told his Corinthian readers that if Jesus was not raised from the dead, we Christians are to be pitied above all others because we are living hope on the basis of a lie (1 Cor 15:19). Some Christians either ignore this one miracle or deny it as a miracle, preferring to interpret it naturalistically as the "rise of faith in the hearts and minds of the disciples." In other words, they claim to believe in the "resurrection" without an empty tomb. That's impossible, however, given the New Testament gospel. It all depends on the empty tomb.

Many modern people struggle with the idea of miracles, but to deny them entirely is to miss the gospel that is based on God's intervention in Jesus Christ including his resurrection. But also, if God exists and is the creator of all, then it would seem miracles must be possible. What kind of God cannot intervene in his own creation? What kind of God would never intervene? And can a nonintervening god be the God of the Bible? Some modern Christians, however, think science is incompatible with belief in miracles, so in order to be modern and consistent with science, they expunge miracles from their Christianity, in which case they are left with a deistic version of Christianity—at best a pale reflection of biblical, orthodox Christianity. What they don't realize is that it does not lie within the purview of science to decide whether miracles happen. Science studies regularities of nature, not irregularities in nature. A miracle should not be thought of as a "violation" of the laws of nature from outside but as God, the author and regulator of nature, using nature's laws differently than usual. The God of traditional Christianity is not "outside of nature" anymore than he is locked within it. Nature is one of God's tools, not a force separate from God. A miracle, then, is not antiscientific; it is extrascientific.

For these and other reasons, Deism is heresy. It reduces the biblical and Christian picture of God to something so small, so insignificant, so banal as to be unimportant. And it can be very dangerous insofar as it leads people to think salvation comes through their own efforts, even if God helps a little (somehow). It is at best a pale reflection of robust, "thick" Christianity. It is at best Christianity that has lost its power. It is negotiated and accommodated Christianity if it is Christianity at all.

Responding to Deism (and MTD)

Christians need to rediscover, without going overboard or to extremes, the God who is involved, who hears and answers prayers, who is both loving and just, and who cannot be captured and tamed. The great Yale theologian H. Richard Niebuhr described the harmless, culturally accommodated god of liberal theology by saying that in that theology "A God without wrath brought men without sin into a kingdom without judgment through the ministrations of a Christ without a cross."[10] That's an apt description of MTD. People too often worry that any mention of God's holiness, justice, and wrath or involvement in history and lives will cause people to jump off the deep end of religion. Someone rightly warned that there's a greater danger than jumping off the deep end and that's jumping off into the shallow end. The problem with Deism, including MTD, is that it is shallow religion.

What is the antidote to Deism and MTD? Christian leaders, including concerned lay people in churches, need to reintroduce a "thick description" of Christianity—biblical, historical, classical Christianity without fanaticism or extremism. We need to rediscover what theologian Karl Barth called "The Strange New World within the Bible" that challenges cultural values and norms and reminds us that God created us in his image and likeness and we must resist all urges to create God in our images. Barth wrote that

> when the gospel is offered to man, and he stretches out his hand to receive it and takes it into his own hand, an acute danger arises which is greater than the danger that he may not understand it and angrily reject it. The danger is that he may accept it peacefully and at once make himself its lord and possessor, thus rendering it innocuous, making that which chooses him something which he himself has chosen, which therefore comes to stand as such alongside all the other things that he can also choose, and therefore control. . . . Wherever the gospel is proclaimed . . . it is exposed at once to the danger of respectability.[11]

Christians need to recover a sense of the countercultural nature of the gospel. The gospel is an offense to common sense and a scandal to ordinary reason. The only way to have it in its full and true reality is to delve deeply into the Bible and Christian history by studying the whole Bible, not just passages that support our values and desires, and all the great voices of the Christian past—especially those who suffered for swimming against the stream of their cultures.

Another tool for recovery from the influence of Deism is to listen to the voices of Christians from non-Western churches and Christian movements. The prevalence of MTD indicates a need for American Christians to receive missionaries from Christian movements in the Global South where Christianity is thriving and, by all account, God's involvement in day-to-day life is evident. They tell us that we, modernized, Western Christians, have pushed God out of the center of our lives and replaced him with individual self-fulfillment, success, national pride, and materialism. We used to send missionaries to them; now perhaps we need them to send missionaries to us! Only they can really point out vividly the ways in which we have subverted the gospel to our culture and thinned it out to where it is a pale reflection of ourselves and our desires.

Throughout the later years of the twentieth century and first decades of the twenty-first century, reported in the previous chapter here, many young Christians have been running away from the shallow, culturally accommodated MTD of much American Christianity toward high Calvinism and divine determinism. They are right to seek a thicker, more challenging, stronger Christian theology that is truly God-centered and in which God is directly involved in the affairs of people. Many others are running toward charismatic television evangelists, "power encounter," "Third Wave" Christianity that revels in supposed miracles. These are fascinated with "spiritual warfare" and the reality of evil forces and powers active in the world. Both of these are reactions to shallow religion exemplified by MTD. Both have their own problems and are unlikely to bring about a real revival of profound biblical and historical Christianity. They tend to attract only certain kinds of people. What is needed is for American churches of all kinds to rediscover God through God's word richly and profoundly proclaimed and applied to daily life.

Bringing It Home

1. Read and discuss 1 Corinthians 15:12-19.

2. Share how God is involved in your daily life. Is God involved and should God be involved with your daily decisions; for example, where you park your car, how you dress, or if you are habitually late to church?

3. What is civil religion? Where do you see it in the community, church, and nation?

4. What do you believe about miracles? Did they happen in the Bible? Have you or someone you know experienced a miracle? Are science and miracles incompatible?

5. How do people settle for a weak, small, and relatively powerless God, when they could experience the God of the Bible? Think about this: How big is my God?

Chapter 10

Using God for Personal Gain

The "Gospel" of Health and Wealth

The Prosperity Heresy of Positive Faith

The previous chapter began with a description of "folk religion." This chapter deals with another facet of modern American folk religion, a heresy that has been exported from America especially to the Global South. It has many names and faces, but most scholars of religion call it the "Prosperity Gospel" and the "Gospel of Health and Wealth" (GHW). It has two main and very different manifestations: (1) a kind of "New Age" positive thinking religion rooted in the nineteenth-century quasireligious movement called "New Thought," and (2) a neo-Pentecostal, charismatic religion touted by television evangelists that revels in miracles. On the surface these two manifestations seem radically different, but below the surface they share much in common. For both, God is a kind of cosmic vending machine who *must* provide health and wealth to all who have "positive faith" expressed in *words of faith*—spoken affirmations or declarations that create reality through divine power. Both treat prayer as magic without realizing it. Both deny God's sovereignty and put God and his power at human disposal. Both elevate health and wealth to the status of ultimate goods. Both claim to be Christian while distorting biblical, historical, classical, orthodox Christianity to the point that it is unrecognizable.

The "New Age" manifestation of this heresy is promoted by various "positive thinking" spiritual gurus influenced by the nineteenth-century

154

movement known as New Thought, which will be described later. It is not Pentecostal or charismatic and often includes belief in reincarnation. Its god is not personal, transcendent, or holy but an impersonal power resident in everything. The human mind is able to tap into it through positive thinking and speaking. The neo-Pentecostal manifestation of this heresy is also influenced by nineteenth-century New Thought, but it is blended with twentieth-century Pentecostalism and charismatic spirituality and heavily influenced by the "divine healing" movement of nineteenth and twentieth-century Christian revivalism. It is closer to orthodox Christianity but takes it in a very different direction through its emphasis on God as guarantor of health and wealth.

I see evidences of this heresy everywhere. One day I saw a billboard near my home that said, "Always wealthy, never poor; Always healthy, never sick—Guaranteed." It was for a new church coming to my neighborhood. I looked up its website and recognized it immediately as a "ministry" of the "Word Faith Movement"—a neo-Pentecostal and charismatic group of churches and revival ministries based on the GHW. I am very familiar with this manifestation of GHW, because I taught theology for two years at a Christian university touched by it. The university's founder, a neo-Pentecostal healing evangelist, was becoming influenced by the GHW while I taught there and many GHW evangelists and ministers spoke in chapel. Many of my students were transfers from a Bible institute in the same city founded by a Pentecostal GHW evangelist and author. Several members of the university's regents were GHW evangelists.

One day in chapel a well-known African-American Pentecostal GHW pastor, televangelist, and author spoke about God's "promise" to reward positive faith, spoken in words "claiming" wealth and health, to supply believers with prosperity and physical wellness. He shouted, "You can't be a witness for Jesus from a wheelchair!" Several of the four thousand students in the chapel were in wheelchairs. A pall fell over the congregation and the evangelist realized his message was not being universally well received. He looked out at the gathering and asked, "Well, am I not right?" One theology professor stood up and shouted, "No!" The chapel broke out in murmuring and muttering of confusion and consternation.

Because of where I was teaching, and the strong presence of neo-Pentecostal GHW teaching in the metropolitan area, I made a point of reading many books both for and against this Word Faith message and theology. I concluded that it is a heresy because of its *emphasis* on something extrabiblical and foreign to classical, historic Christianity and its *distorted image of God.*

Over the years since then, for the past quarter of a century, I have seen the GHW message grow and spread into the Global South—Latin America, Asia, and Africa. Almost every city of any size in North America and those continents have churches dedicated to the GHW. Some of them are of the neo-Pentecostal Word Faith variety and some are of the New Age variety. A few combine features of both. Many television "ministries" promote the GHW. Some seemingly secular talk shows subtly promote the New Age version of it. Numerous books crowding the shelves of even secular bookstores promote it. It has become so widespread and influential that it seems inescapable.

The GHW goes beyond mere "positive thinking" to claiming that it is possible to gain health and wealth by "naming and claiming it" (as some advocates describe the process). The power that brings health and wealth to the person is God's, but the means of accessing that power is the individual's. Most often the technique for accessing God's power for health and wealth ("abundance") is use of spoken affirmations such as "I am a child of the King [God] and possess perfect abundance. All that is God's is mine. I am well and rich." Some GHW evangelists teach followers to "confront God with his promises" and "claim health and wealth" as your own. Merely thinking positive thoughts isn't enough; GHW advocates teach that instead one must speak health and wealth into existence. Positive speaking will attract abundance. Some call this the "law of attraction."

Why the GHW Is Heresy

Various versions of the GHW have become so common and widespread that many people take them for granted as part of their spiritualities, including many Christians. Entire churches specialize in the GHW and are often known as "Unity" (the New Age version of the GHW) or "Word Faith" (the neo-Pentecostal/charismatic version). However, numerous independent churches with no giveaway name specialize in the GHW. So why call this a heresy if it is so popular and widespread? Well, of course, as I have already argued throughout this book, whether something is or isn't a heresy cannot be decided by how popular it is. The GHW is heresy because it takes one small aspect of biblical revelation, distorts it, elevates it to part of the gospel, and treats God as a "vending machine" instead of as the holy, transcendent, sovereign Lord of creation. It also offers false hope to people facing illness and poverty and at least *implies* that those result from lack of faith. It blames victims for their own wretchedness. Finally, it confuses prayer with magic and faith with presumption.

Of course, as already noted, the GHW comes in many varieties and degrees of emphasis on health and wealth. Here I am focusing only on those "ministries" that make these central to the gospel itself and teach that "true faith," spoken in the right manner, *always* brings health and wealth from God because God wants all of his people to be perfectly healthy and financially prosperous and has promised these blessings as rewards for true faith "guaranteed."

Does God promise his people health and wealth as a reward for true faith—guaranteed? Most GHW teachers focus on a few verses from the Bible as proof texts for their message. One is Jeremiah 29:11: "I know the plans I have in mind for you, declares the LORD; they are plans for peace, not disaster, to give you a future filled with hope." Some English translations, including the New International Version, say "plans to prosper you." The Hebrew is unclear; it can be translated in several ways. Advocates of the GHW prefer "plans to prosper you" and quote it often. Another proof text often used by GHW believers is Malachi 3:10: "Bring the whole tenth-part to the storage house . . . test me in this, says the LORD of heavenly forces. See whether I do not open all the windows of the heavens for you and empty out a blessing until there is enough." This verse is especially popular among advocates of "Seed Faith"—an extension of the GHW that emphasizes giving money to Christian ministries with the promise of financial reward.

Two New Testament passages are often used by GHW preachers and teachers to support their theology. John 10:10 quotes Jesus: "The thief comes only to steal and kill and destroy. I came that they may have life, and have it abundantly" (NRSV). GHW promoters interpret "abundant life" as including perfect health and financial prosperity. Third John 2 says "Dear friend, I'm praying that all is well with you and that you enjoy good health in the same way that you prosper spiritually." A favorite translation of this verse among GHW believers is "Beloved, I wish above all things that thou mayest prosper and be in health, even as thy soul prospereth" (KJV). As with Jeremiah 29:11, however, the Greek of 3 John 2 does not require the translation "prosper" and certainly does not require any reference to financial prosperity.

The entire GHW rests almost solely on these four Bible passages—and on personal testimonies, evangelegends (stories told by religious people without any proof), and New Thought philosophy (which will be explained in the next section). I say "almost" because there can be real doubt that scripture teaches that God ideally wills poverty and illness. But a distinction must be recognized between God's ideal or "antecedent will," what God wishes were the case, and God's permissive or "consequent will," what God allows because of humanity's sinful condition. Much of scripture points to God's will for people to experience "life abundant," but that is either presently spiritual (sins forgiven, right relationship with God) or eschatological—what will be the case in the future kingdom of God. Believers in the GHW interpret this theme of scripture physically and already (as opposed to "not yet").

Overall, scripture does not reveal that God guarantees or even always wills even the godliest people's physical health and financial prosperity. One example is the Apostle Paul who confessed that he suffered a "thorn in [his] body" that God refused to remove—even though he prayed for it to be removed (2 Cor 12). He even considered it *from God*. GHW advocates say that Paul's thorn in the flesh was not a physical ailment but something like persecution or rebellion against his ministry by some of his converts. That is not, however, exegetically likely. Most scholars believe Paul suffered from poor eyesight based on his need for an amanuensis (secretary or scribe). Many of God's most faithful prophets and human instruments (in biblical times and afterward) suffered great physical torment and poverty.

One scripture passage some GHW believers claim on their side is James 5:13-15, where the author (possibly Jesus's brother) instructs Christians to have "elders" anoint the sick with oil and pray for them and promises that the Lord will "restore them to health." The passage says nothing, however, about "claiming" health or prosperity. It doesn't even mention the faith of the sick person! And it is much to be doubted that this is an unconditional promise; if it were, no person prayed for by faithful elders with oil anointing would ever die!

But more important than the very slight, if existent at all, biblical evidence for the GHW is the Bible's emphasis on "life abundant" as gospel liberty—being made free from guilt and bondage to sin and the law by God's grace. The gospel is not about physical health and financial prosperity; it is about God's mercy, forgiveness, and inward transformation into the likeness of Jesus Christ. That God sometimes heals people in response to prayer (or unilaterally out of compassion) is not part of the gospel; it is simply a gift of

God. To import it or financial prosperity into the gospel is to shift the focus of the gospel away from God and onto the human being. And it raises doubts about God's forgiveness of sins when physical healing or financial prosperity are not forthcoming in response to true faith.

I once knew a Pentecostal minister who suffered terribly from a blood clotting disease that threatened his life. He had several embolisms that went to his lungs and had to be removed in emergency surgeries. He prayed fervently and with faith that God would heal him. His family and congregation and wide circle of friends prayed for his healing—"claiming" it as God's promise (as they believed). His entire denomination prayed for him. When he was not healed he began doubting his salvation. That's the logical outcome of making physical healing or financial prosperity part of the gospel itself.

My own mother, a Pentecostal minister's wife and strong believer in physical healing through prayer, died alone in the hospital at age thirty-two, because my father and our church and denomination believed she would be healed and ignored the signs of her impending death. She was to be prayed for by a world-famous "faith healing" evangelist the next week. My family and church believed so strongly that she would be healed that they did not linger at her bedside as she declined.

As I will discuss in the next section, "healing in the atonement" is a Pentecostal doctrine that lies in the background of the GHW—especially its Pentecostal and neo-Pentecostal advocates. I was raised to believe that just as Christ's death on the cross secured salvation for those who repent and believe (trust in Christ alone), so his death on the cross secured physical healing for all who have faith to be healed. This opened wide the door to the GHW when it began to take off in the 1970s through certain Pentecostal "ministries." Early in my theological education, however, I saw the danger in this as mentioned above. If God's promise to forgive in response to faith is unconditional and so is God's promise to heal, then someone who remains ill in spite of faith and prayer may not be saved either. No Pentecostal (or other group that believes in divine healing through prayer) says this, but the logic is inexorable. I'm sure the Pentecostal minister in the above anecdote was not the first or only one to doubt his salvation because he was not healed. (He eventually died of his disease doubting his salvation.)

Another reason the GHW is heresy is that it treats God like a vending machine rather than as the holy, sovereign Lord of all. According to GHW preachers and teachers, God is obligated to heal and provide financial prosperity to those who approach him in faith, by which they mean "name it and claim it." A student who was a passionate believer in the GHW once told me that he "confronts God with his promises" when he needs healing or money. This view of God, that God must heal and prosper, is common among GHW evangelists. They teach their followers how to experience healing and prosperity through confronting God with his promises and through true faith by which they mean *acting as if the promise is already fulfilled*. I have personally known GHW believers who have thrown away their badly needed glasses, crutches, and medicines. Others have purchased expensive cars—beyond what they could afford. True faith, they believed, is incompatible with depending on living as sick or poor. The "law of attraction" encourages this—physical wellness and financial prosperity are "attracted" to a person by acting as if they are already one's possession. It's difficult to find this explicitly taught in GHW writings, but many GHW believers have heard it taught in their churches and by television evangelists.

All of that is treating God like a vending machine into which one deposits "true faith" and out of which must come physical wellness and financial prosperity. Instead, the God of the Bible is sovereign and cannot be manipulated. Some of the Hebrew people thought that God had to bless them simply because they were his "chosen people." They interpreted God's promises of blessing as unconditional. The prophets criticized this attitude as did Jesus. First Samuel 15:22 and Hosea 6:6 both report God as saying that he desires "mercy" more than "sacrifice." God did not bless and prosper his people when they disobeyed through idolatry or spiritual indifference or oppression of the poor among them. All of God's promises are conditional and God remains free; God cannot be manipulated into doing anything. To think he can be is to trivialize God and put him at the mercy of creatures. It is a poor and pathetic view of God.

Yet another reason the GHW is heresy is that it offers false hope to desperate people. The plain fact of the matter is that followers of the GHW die at the same rate as other people—one death per person. Even the founders and leaders of the movements (Pentecostal version and New Age version) have died. All died of some illness—whether their followers call it that or not. When the leading Pentecostal GHW leader died in old age his followers boasted that he had never been ill a day in his life—since his conversion and healing as an adolescent. Critics naturally scoffed at that claim and pointed to the day he died! Even if he simply expired without pain his death was caused by some illness. What was written on his death certificate? "Death by no cause?" Not likely. A common diagnosis of death in old age is "cardiogenic shock," which is medical jargon for "heart failure." Followers of the GHW *may* live healthier and more financially prosperous lives than their non-GHW counterparts. I know of no study that shows that they do or do not. However, studies have shown that having a positive attitude can affect physical well-being and financial prosperity—up to a point. But it alone cannot cure cancer or delay death indefinitely or pay off expensive cars bought on credit without sufficient income to repay.

The GHW is extremely popular among poorer segments of society. That's understandable. And it's understandable when a person with a terminal illness turns to it for hope. The problem is that it does not really deliver what it promises. The sign I saw near my home that promoted a GHW church saying, "Always wealthy, never poor. Always healthy, never sick—guaranteed," is simply a false promise. Scripture doesn't make it and people who believe in it are always eventually disappointed. It's simply cruel to hold out false hope to people and that is what the GHW does.

Yet another reason the GHW is heresy is closely connected with the preceding one: the GHW necessarily, logically blames the victims of illness and poverty for their conditions. Most GHW preachers and teachers would not say it quite as blatantly as the television evangelist who proclaimed, "You cannot be a good witness for Jesus from a wheelchair," but that is logically implied in the belief system itself. If physical healing is guaranteed by God in response to true faith, then a person who is not healed must not be exercising true faith. If financial prosperity is guaranteed by God in response to true faith, then a person experiencing poverty must not be exercising truth faith. The logic is ironclad, even if most promoters of the GHW are reluctant to follow it. So what do GHW teachers say when faith-filled followers are not healed or continue to experience poverty? Usually they encourage them to "persevere in faith" and keep "claiming it" until health or financial blessing appear. After a time, however, something else must be said—especially when the GHW believer who continues in illness or poverty demonstrates strong, true faith by "naming and claiming" it. Then, often, the GHW promoter blames the suffering person's family, friends, and/or faith community. Someone besides God must be responsible. Some Pentecostals will blame Satan and even encourage spoken declarations against Satan such as "Satan, get your hands off this suffering person!" (I once taught at a Christian university where many chapel speakers were promoters of the GHW and sometimes heard them speaking to Satan more than to God!) Whatever dodge they may use, however, to relieve the sufferer of blame, the logic of the GHW forces the blame back on the person suffering. He or she will naturally conclude that the suffering is due to his or her lack of true faith.

Finally, the GHW is heresy because it treats *prayer* as *magic* and *faith* as *presumption*. These points tie closely with the previous one about God being sovereign. It is absolutely essential to recognize the difference between prayer and magic. Here "magic" does not mean "parlor tricks" or what Las Vegas celebrity magicians perform for audiences. Here "magic" is being used in its more technical sense—as any technique for manipulating reality through paranormal means. (Some practitioners of this add *k* to the end of the word, thus *magick*, to distinguish it from entertainment tricks of illusion.) Magic, or magick, in this sense, is not prayer. Prayer is asking God to do something; it recognizes God's sovereignty alongside God's power. It does not attempt to manipulate God and as soon as it does it becomes magick rather than prayer.

The "law of attraction," when put into practice, is a form of magick. It is based on the idea that, for example, acting a certain way such as well or prosperous will automatically attract wellness or prosperity to the acting person. Many self-help gurus and "success-motivation" seminars teach some form of this. It may help, but it's not prayer. Many New Age people call their meditation practices "prayer" when they do not include belief in a personal God. That's a misuse of the word *prayer*. Often the meditation practices are actually forms of magick. Again, they may help, but they are not prayer. "Name it and claim it" is magick even if it is labeled *prayer*. It is an attempt to gain power even over God—to force God to keep his alleged promises. It attempts to manipulate God. Prayer that ends with "your will be done" is never wrong and yet many GHW teachers discourage such. They say that ending prayer that way weakens its force. That proves their idea of prayer is really turning prayer into magick. Any attempt to gain power over God is almost by definition heresy if not blasphemy.

One might wonder about some prayers in the Bible. Didn't Moses, for example, wrestle with God in prayer, arguing with God about the Hebrew people and what God planned to do to them because of their idolatry? Yes, but through it all Moses recognized God's authority, freedom, and sovereignty. He never questioned God's right to do what he saw fit and he never attempted to manipulate God. Arguing with God is not wrong; it does not constitute magick. The line from prayer into magick is crossed as soon as one attempts to force God's hand through manipulative words that allegedly *cause* God to do something. Then God is being treated as an impersonal force or power, which is how magick conceives of ultimate reality.

Another all-important distinction is between faith and presumption. Faith is in essence trust; presumption is in essence distrust. In its biblical sense, faith in God is trust in God to be good and wise. Presumption is always evidence of distrust in someone's goodness. To "presume" in a relationship is to step over a boundary and impose one's own will because one does not trust the other person's good will or wisdom. For example, a common saying that expresses and justifies presumption is "It's always easier to get forgiveness than permission." To act on that principle in a network of relationships (family, organization, etc.) is to act presumptuously. It is to presume that one's own will is more important than others'. It is to presume that one's own wisdom or desire trumps others'. Presumption is the opposite of faith. To show faith in a network of relationships (or a one-on-one relationship) is to trust others' good will and wisdom.

Sometimes presumption is better than faith—such as when one knows that the other person does not have good will or wisdom and one knows his or her own course of action is better than what the other would permit. However, in relation to God, presumption is always an insult to God's goodness and wisdom. In that relationship, faith as trust is always appropriate and presumption is always inappropriate because of who God is. To *ask* God for something such as healing or prosperity with faith is to recognize God's greater wisdom and leave room for God to say "no" (as in the Apostle Paul's case with regard to his thorn in the flesh and in the case of Jesus praying in the Garden of Gethsemane). Presumption appears as soon as one treats prayer as a means of manipulating God. It appears whenever prayer leaves behind trust in God and attempts to cause God to do something. Presumption also appears when one acts a certain way in order to "attract" God's power. Then presumption and magick merge.

The evidence that the GHW is heresy, in the sense described at the beginning of the previous chapter, is overwhelming. Of course, there are beliefs and teachings about health and wealth that are not heretical. The Bible encourages, or at least does not forbid, desiring well-being and asking God for it. And there is strong evidence that God does *wish* his people to be well, but that is a far cry from believing that God *must* provide health and wealth to everyone who has faith for them. The factors that make the GHW heresy are *focus* and *emphasis*. People often tell me, "But there's truth in it." What they mean is simply that positive thinking and praying for well-being are good. But the GHW goes much further than garden-variety positive thinking and faithful praying. It crosses a line between biblical orthodoxy and heresy whenever it places health and wealth at the center of the gospel and Christian living, treats God as an object for manipulation, treats prayer as magick and encourages presumption (e.g., throwing away much-needed medicine), or implies that the ill or poor are to blame for their conditions.

The History of the GHW

So where did the GHW come from? How did it arise to such prominence so that many, if not most, television evangelists promote it? Why are Christian and even secular bookstore shelves crammed with books promoting some version of it? Why are whole churches devoted to it?

There are no simple, easy answers to those questions. However, one can study and understand the genesis of the GHW and trace its development in American religious life. Predictably its origins lie along the margins of American religion—in certain cults and new religious sects that appeared in the nineteenth century and early twentieth century.

Beginning in the middle of the nineteenth century a New England-based philosopher named Phineas Parkhurst Quimby (d. 1866) began teaching that positive thinking could heal a person of virtually any illness. He taught that the power of God resided in the individual through faith, which he treated as positive thinking. He became the first "practitioner" of what later came to be known as "New Thought"—a distinctly American quasireligious philosophy of "mind over matter." According to Quimby and his followers, the human mind is able to tap into the infinite power of God through positive thinking. One of his most famous "patients" was Mary Baker Eddy, founder of the Church of Christ, Scientist ("Christian Science"). Eddy believed she was healed of a terrible illness through Quimby's therapy that had mainly to do with positive thinking.

Eddy, who died in 1910, founded her church in Boston and it is still the "Mother Church" of the entire Christian Science movement worldwide. She wrote a commentary on the Bible entitled *Science and Health with a Key to the Scriptures* that expresses her Quimby-based interpretation of Christianity that focused on physical healing. For her and her followers, matter is illusion, so sickness and death are not really real. "There is no sin, sickness, or death" is a popular Christian Science saying. Sin, sickness, and death *happen*, but their *happening* is illusion. If the mind were capable of denying them strongly enough, they would have no reality or power. The denial of sin, sickness, and death is "faith" and the positive thinking that leads away from their illusion toward perfect realization of God who is "All," the "Mind of the Universe," the only being who really exists, is "prayer."

Christian Science became very popular in the late nineteenth century and remained so throughout much of the twentieth century. Its popularity declined toward the end of the twentieth century although it still exists as a denomination. Many conservative Christians call it a "cult," but it is not that in the popular media sense. Most Christian Scientists are older, middle-class Caucasians. Many of them are highly educated.

Christian Science, however, is probably not the most influential form of New Thought. Though probably smaller in number of members, the Unity School of Christianity (or simply "Unity") arose around the same time as Christian Science and gained a very large following. Many people influenced by Unity never join a Unity church or fellowship, but at least one exists in virtually every city of America.

Unity was founded in the late nineteenth century by two New Thought believers and practitioners named Charles and Myrtle Fillmore. Like Mary Baker Eddy, they combined Quimby's New Thought philosophy and healing therapy with Christianity. Unlike Eddy and Christian Science, they did not deny the reality of matter or sin, sickness, and death, but they did believe strongly in mind over matter and added financial prosperity to Christian Science's emphasis on healing. Over the decades Unity blossomed into a kind of transdenominational positive thinking movement, although it has churches without exclusive membership. (People can be members of other churches and often are.) The Fillmores and Unity added to Quimby's and Eddy's New Thought emphasis on mind over matter the practice of speaking positive "affirmations" that would, so they claimed, attract health and prosperity. An example of a Unity affirmation is "God is my source; I claim abundant good." Such affirmations are often printed on small cards and kept in a box on a Unity person's kitchen or dining room table—much like evangelical Protestant "promise boxes" that were common in Christian homes in the past. Christian "promise boxes," however, typically contained scripture verses; Unity affirmations are usually positive declarations that, when repeated with faith, attract health and prosperity. They are a form of magick (although Unity people would not call them that).

Many Unity churches and fellowships became havens for Christians influenced by the New Age Movement in the 1970s and 1980s. They brought with them belief in reincarnation, which Unity allows. The New Age Movement was a great stimulus to Unity growth. Unity's idea of God, however, is unorthodox. To Unity, God is the "Mind" of the universe, present in all beings whose power for good is infinite and always available to positive thought and speech. Whether God is personal in Unity's theology is debatable. Certainly God is not the orthodox Trinity of Father, Son, and Holy Spirit. To Unity and other New Thought groups Jesus is the ultimate teacher and practitioner of faith and prayer—interpreted as positive thinking and speaking.

New Thought is the background source of what I earlier called the New Age form of the GHW. It is non-Pentecostal and less well-known than Pentecostal and charismatic GHW because the latter is represented by many or most television evangelists.

The "guru" of Pentecostal GHW was healing evangelist E. W. Kenyon (d. 1948). Kenyon was deeply involved in the late nineteenth and early twentieth-century "divine healing movement" among evangelical Christians. Beginning in the middle of the nineteenth century and growing throughout the next century was a plethora of "Holiness" (revivalistic offshoots of Methodism) and Pentecostal evangelists who prayed for the sick and believed in miracles of physical healing. Among the notable ones were A. B. Simpson, founder of the Christian and Missionary Alliance denomination; Aimee Semple McPherson, founder of the Pentecostal Church of the Foursquare Gospel; William Branham, Oral Roberts, T. L. Osborn, and Kathryn Kuhlman. These healing evangelists were, by and large, orthodox Christians who believed that physical healing was provided in Christ's atonement and that God wanted to and would heal when people prayed for healing with faith. They all also claimed (or their followers claimed for them) possession of the "gift of healing" mentioned in 1 Corinthians 12. Thousands, perhaps millions, of sick people and their loved ones flocked to "healing crusades" held in tents and auditoriums. Oral Roberts founded a Christian university with a hospital where he attempted to "merge prayer and medicine."

Kenyon believed there was some truth in New Thought and attempted to unite it and Holiness-Pentecostal healing ministry. His numerous books contain elements of New Thought, but his overall theology was orthodox. He believed in the Trinity and unique deity of Christ. However, he popularized among Holiness-Pentecostal believers the New Thought idea that true faith must be spoken and that speaking healing and prosperity could create them. Kenyon's message did not "catch fire," so to speak, among the masses. But it did introduce healing evangelists to the Unity and New Thought message and many of them began to absorb aspects of New Thought into their teaching about prayer and prosperity.

The person who really launched the Pentecostal GHW movement, also known as the "Word Faith Movement" (WFM) was Kenneth Hagin Sr. (d. 2003), who founded the Rhema Bible School, which grew to thousands of students in Tulsa, Oklahoma. Through him and his ministry and the ministries of Oral Roberts and T. L. Osborn, Tulsa became the "headquarters" of the Pentecostal GHW.

Hagin started out as an Assemblies of God minister and evangelist. (The Assemblies of God is a large "mainline" Pentecostal denomination that came to repudiate the GHW.) Later he adopted Kenyon's blend of New Thought and Pentecostal divine healing theology and started the WFM. The WFM is nearly synonymous with Hagin and his followers. Some critics have claimed that Hagin plagiarized some of his writings about faith, health, and prosperity, especially the emphasis on speaking the "Word of Faith," from Kenyon. Hagin himself, however, denied it and attributed the similarities to common inspiration and discovery. There can be no doubt, however, that Kenyon's and Hagin's theologies were very similar.

Hagin taught (and his son and successor teaches) that God wants every one of his people, Christians, to live in perfect health and financial prosperity. And the path to experiencing these blessings is positive "Word Faith"—speaking them into existence. Many of his followers practice this by living *as if* they are already healthy and prosperous—implying the law of attraction.

Perhaps better known than Hagin, however, is his follower (also Oral Roberts's follower) Kenneth Copeland who, together with his wife Gloria, hosts a television program, writes books about the Word Faith message of healing and financial prosperity, and speaks at large conferences. Hagin, Copeland, and the numerous Pentecostal evangelists inspired by them attract millions of people worldwide to the GHW and into the WFM.

During the last decade of the twentieth century and first decades of the twenty-first century, a new promoter of a mild version of the GHW appeared on the scene and is probably the most famous of all: Joel Osteen, pastor of Lakewood Church of Houston, Texas, the largest Protestant church in the United States. Osteen succeeded his father as pastor of Pentecostal Lakewood Church and built it up to be the mother of all megachurches. His sermons are televised; he is a frequent guest on secular talk shows, and his face is familiar to almost all Americans. His books are numerous and well advertised. Many of them are bestsellers—even to non-Christian readers. The gospel Osteen preaches and promotes is one of personal well-being and success, including physical wellness, through positive thinking. The New Thought strain is noticeable in his messages although his theology is orthodox by historical Christian standards. Critics say the problem is the *emphasis* he places on personal success and well-being through positive thinking and speaking at the expense of self-sacrifice, suffering for Christ (and with the sick and poor), and growth in holiness.

It is no exaggeration to say that New Thought is a distinctly American quasireligious philosophy that has permeated American culture. Its influence can be seen everywhere. It is optimistic and practical—two features that are notably American. Pentecostalism is also a distinctly American spiritual movement. What brings the two together is their common emphasis on *faith* and *healing*. However, historical Pentecostalism did not interpret faith as magick; the Word Faith version of Pentecostalism at least flirts with it and that comes from its encounter with New Thought in Kenyon. Most of the mainline Pentecostal denominations have criticized the WFM and the GHW. Nevertheless, those have filtered in even where they are not welcome. Numerous Pentecostal churches have divided and split over the GHW—spawning new independent Word Faith churches.

Responding to the Gospel of Health and Wealth

"I was there." It's a common saying among people who live long enough to look back at the beginning of a movement and describe its birth and growth. I was there when the GHW and the WFM was spreading rapidly among Pentecostals and charismatics in the 1970s. In fact, I was there before that. As a young Bible college student I often listened to Kenneth Hagin on the radio; his "Faith Seminar of the Air" was fascinating if nothing else. During my seminary years (1975–78) I served on the pastoral staff of an independent Pentecostal church that struggled with the GHW and the WFM. Several followers of Hagin and Copeland and other WFM evangelists attempted to insert the GHW into the church through adult Sunday school classes and home Bible study groups. Then a WFM graduate of Rhema Bible Institute came to town and started a WFM church. Many of our church's people fascinated with the GHW went there. After studying theology in Germany (1982) I took a position teaching theology at Oral Roberts University—an ecumenical neo-Pentecostal schools of arts and sciences and graduate schools. During my two years on its faculty, I constantly battled the GHW in my classes—as did most of the faculty. Chapel speakers, however, often promoted it and the founder-president and his son seemed to be drawing closer to it all the time. I left just when they were joining a new WFM church. (Oral himself grew up Pentecostal and made his reputation as a healing evangelist as one, but for about a decade before I arrived at his university, he was Methodist.)

I have probably never been asked a single question more often than how to deal with the GHW. During my thirty-two years of teaching in three Christian universities I have encountered numerous students and church members touched by the GHW who wanted my advice. My advice has always been to run from it as far and as fast as possible. On the surface it can sound good, but underneath it is pernicious. Because many of its promoters and practitioners are truly "born again" and Jesus-loving Christians, people are reluctant to believe the message itself is dangerous or seriously mistaken.

Pastors and lay leaders of Christian churches need to take a firm stand against the GHW in all its forms without throwing the baby of God's benevolent will—even for physical healing—out with the bathwaters of distorted emphasis and magick and presumption. Overreaction is not called for. That God wants to heal the sick and does not want people to starve or live in dehumanizing poverty is true; many churches need to discover or recover that truth. Prayer for the sick is biblical, but presumptuous "faith" is counterfeit faith. A strong emphasis on the sovereignty of God is called for in response to the GHW and the WFM and New Thought.

Bringing It Home

1. Read, study, and discuss Jeremiah 29:11; Malachi 3:10; John 10:10; and 2 Corinthians 12. What kind of life does God want us to have? What is the difference between peace and wholeness and physical and economic well-being?

2. Describe the distinction between asking God and demanding or claiming something from God. In your experience, is God a kind of vending machine?

3. Why do some people find the Gospel of Health and Wealth so attractive? How might GHW rob people of hope? Why might GHW be so popular in other parts of the world?

4. Perhaps you have heard people say, "Name it and claim it." How might you respond when the wish is not granted?

5. Having a positive attitude is a good thing, but bad things happen despite and sometimes because of a person's faith. How does GHW offer false hope? Can you be a Christian witness from a wheelchair? Do you know some people who are witnesses despite or even because of their illnesses or disabilities?

Conclusion

Many well-meaning people, Christians included, consider any talk of "heresy" tantamount to "religious McCarthyism"—that is, as intolerant and leading toward persecution. For about fifteen years, while teaching theology and religious studies at a Christian university, I taught a course on "America's Cults and New Religions." Because of my interest in and knowledge of cults and new religions I was invited to speak to many church groups in the metropolitan area where the university was located. Occasionally, while explaining to an adult Sunday school class or church "Adult Forum" why a certain new religion was not Christian and possibly even dangerous to people's spiritual if not physical health and well-being, I was harshly criticized for being intolerant. My frequent answer was that tolerance does not require agreement with everything or even lack of legitimate criticism. Also, if Christianity is compatible with anything and everything, it is literally nothing.

There are, to be sure, Christian "anticultists" who thrive, even make a living, on discovering theological error and heresy where nobody has before noticed it. Fundamentalist Christians overaccuse everyone but themselves of serious error and even heresy. The beliefs I have here labeled heresy do not make their adherents evil or dangerous—except perhaps to people's spiritual well-being. Ideas have consequences and Christianity has cognitive content. Being Christian implies believing certain things. The ideas I have criticized as heresies here are ones the vast majority of mainline Christians of all denominations have looked at, considered, and declared outside the pale of Christian orthodoxy. That is by no means to suggest the people who believe them ought to be persecuted. It is to suggest that Christian leaders and teachers ought to correct them.

171

At the heart of Christianity lies the gospel—good news to all people and especially those suffering from guilt and despair. The good news is that God has acted to reconcile them to himself through Jesus Christ and give them hope. All the heresies described here undermine that good news in some way. All of them twist and distort it into a "different gospel" that does not speak real hope into people's lives and does not bring reconciliation between them and God.

Christians ought to have compassion on those affected by what one Christian author has rightly labeled "the cruelty of heresy." Heresy is not just wrong thinking; it is false gospel and therefore no gospel at all. My hope is that Christian readers will teach fellow Christians about the true gospel and warn them against these false gospels—by speaking the truth in love.

Bringing It Home

1. Reflect on your reading. What did you learn? What surprised you?

2. What are the basic Christian beliefs? Can you believe anything you want and still be a Christian?

3. Talk about tolerance and the limits of tolerance. Most people have no trouble expressing their intolerance for something they feel strongly about. Are we really willing to accept any belief and find it an acceptable basis for our faith? What is the value of having standards and boundaries? When does criticism become a "witch hunt"?

4. What is the important takeaway from this book for you?

Notes

2. Understanding *Orthodoxy*

1. Irenaeus, *Irenaeus against Heresies* 1.10 in vol. 1 of *The Ante-Nicene Fathers: The Apostolic Fathers with Justin Martyr and Irenaeus*, ed. Alexander Roberts and James Donaldson (Grand Rapids, MI: Eerdmans, 1985), 330–331.

2. Tertullian, *On Prescription against Heretics* 2.13 in vol. 3 of *The Ante-Nicene Fathers: Latin Christianity: Its Founder, Tertullian*, ed. Alexander Roberts and James Donaldson (Grand Rapids, MI: Eerdmans, 1986), 249.

3. Some readers will want to know about the supposed difference between Roman Catholic and Protestant theologies of salvation. Catholic theology teaches the orthodox belief that salvation is solely by God's grace. God's grace is the one and only efficient cause of salvation. However, "works of love" are, along with faith, necessary as an "instrumental cause" of salvation. The Protestant reformers thought this tended to undermine salvation by grace alone, so they coined the phrase "salvation by grace alone through faith alone." The Catholic Church accepts the "grace alone" part but rejects the "faith alone" part. For Catholics, salvation is by grace alone through faith made active in works of love. But Protestants also believe saving grace always produces works of love. So, during the later decades of the twentieth century and first decade of the twenty-first century many Catholic and Protestant leaders took steps toward overcoming that part of the division between Catholics and Protestants arguing it is a semantic difference. However, so long as Catholics continue to talk about "merit" attached to good works, some Protestants will hold back from believing they really mean salvation is "by grace alone." Nevertheless, Catholics insist that even merit is a product of grace, not of human effort alone.

4. G. E. Lessing, "On the Proof of the Spirit and Power," *Lessing's Theological Writings*, ed. Henry Chadwick (Stanford, CA: Stanford University Press, 1956), 51–56.

5. John Calvin, *Institutes of the Christian Religion*, book 1, trans. Ford Lewis Battles, ed. John T. McNeill (Philadelphia, PA: Westminster Press, 1960), 74.

6. Quoted in Lawrence A. Hoffman, *The Art of Public Prayer: Not for Clergy Alone* (Skylight Paths Publishing, 1999), 31.

3. The Mother of All Heresies

1. This story about John told by Polycarp is reported by Irenaeus, Polycarp's disciple and bishop of Lyons, in *Irenaeus against Heresies* 3.3 in vol. 1 of *The Ante-Nicene Fathers*, 416.

2. *Irenaeus against Heresies* 4.20 in vol. 1 of *The Ante-Nicene Fathers*, 490.

3. Albert E. Brumley, "I'll Fly Away" (Hartford Music Company, 1932; Albert E. Brumley and Sons, 1960).

4. Helen H. Lemmel, "Turn Your Eyes Upon Jesus" (1922, Singspiration Music, 1950).

4. Messing with Divine Revelation

1. Friedrich Schleiermacher, *The Christian Faith*, ed. H. R. Mackintosh and J. S. Stewart (Philadelphia, PA: Fortress Press, 1976), 608.

2. These were first published in "Testing the New Prophets," *Christianity Today* (January 14, 1991).

5. Doubting the Deity of Jesus Christ

1. Technically, the slogan was, "There was when the Son was not," but clearly it meant the Son of God was created in time by God the Father.

2. Gregory of Nazianzus, "To Cledonius the Priest against Apollinarius," *The Nicene and Post-Nicene Fathers, Second Series*, vol. 7, ed. Philip Schaff and Henry Wace (Grand Rapids, MI: Eerdmans, 1983), 440.

3. Letter of Pope Leo the Great to Flavian, Bishop of Constantinople (449).

4. *The United Methodist Hymnal* (Nashville: The United Methodist Publishing House, 1989), 14.

6. Contesting the Trinity

1. See Gary Kinkel, *Our Dear Mother the Spirit: An Investigation of Count Zinzendorf's Theology and Praxis* (Lanham, MD: University Press of America, 1990), 79–131.

7. Setting Grace Aside

1. Some will argue that Augustine always believed in free will but came to define free will as compatible with determinism. The point here is only that he denied sinners' ability, even under the pressure of prevenient grace, to resist or accept saving grace without the efficacious grace of God. In other words, he embraced irresistible grace and redefined free will in that light. For him, in his later writings, "free will" is only doing what you want to do—not being able to do otherwise.

2. Whether John Wesley was influenced directly by Arminius is debatable, but he named his magazine *The Arminian*, so he clearly was influenced by Arminius even if only indirectly.

3. Bruce R. McConkie, *Mormon Doctrine*, 2nd ed. (Salt Lake City, UT: Bookcraft, 1979), 671.

4. James E. Talmage, *A Study of the Articles of Faith*, 12th ed. (Salt Lake City, UT: 1971), 107.

5. Ibid., 404.

6. See also ibid., 89.

8. Making God a Monster

1. *On Grace and Free Will* in vol. 5 of *The Nicene and Post-Nicene Fathers: St. Augustine: Anti-Pelagian Writings*, series 1, ed. Philip Schaff (Grand Rapids, MI: Eerdmans, 1988), 41.

2. Ibid., 45.

3. Ulrich Zwingli, *On Providence and Other Essays*, ed. William John Hinke (Durham, NC: Labyrinth Press, 1983), 176.

4. Ibid., 182.

5. Ibid.

6. Ibid.

7. Ibid.

8. Ibid., 176.

9. Ibid., 186–187.

10. John Calvin, *Calvin: Institutes of the Christian Religion*, trans. Ford Lewis Battles, ed. John T. McNeill, vol. 1 (Louisville: Westminster John Knox, 1960), 229.

11. Ibid., 209.

12. Ibid.

13. Ibid., 234.

14. Ibid., 235.

15. Jonathan Edwards, *The Works of Jonathan Edwards, A.M.*, vol. 1 (London: William Ball, Paternoster Row, 1839), 106.

16. Jonathan Edwards, *Sermons of Jonathan Edwards* (Peabody MA: Hendrickson Publishers, 2005), 162.

17. Ibid.

18. Ibid., 164.

19. Edwards, *The Works of Jonathan Edwards*, 87.

20. Ibid., 76.

21. R. C. Sproul, *What Is Reformed Theology? Understanding the Basics* (Grand Rapids: Baker Books, 1997), 121.

22. Ibid., 172.

23. Ibid., 132.

24. John Piper, "Why I Do Not Say, 'God Did Not Cause the Calamity, but He Can Use It for Good,'" *Desiring God*, September 17, 2001, http://www.desiringgod.org/articles/why-i-do-not-say-god-did-not-cause-the-calamity-but-he-can-use-it-for-good.

25. John Wesley, *The Works of the Reverend John Wesley, A. M.*, vol. 6 (New York: J. Emory and B. Waugh, 1831), 41.

9. Reducing God to Manageable Size

1. Quoted in Kenda Creasy Dean, *Almost Christian: What the Faith of Our Teenagers Is Telling the American Church* (Oxford: Oxford University Press, 2010), 3. By permission of Oxford University Press, USA.

2. Ibid., 14.

3. Ibid.

4. Ibid.

5. See John Pindar Bland, *President Roosevelt and Paine's Defamers* (Boston, MA: Boston Investigation Co., 1903), 9.

6. Ibid., 5.

7. Ibid.

8. Michael Card, "I Have Decided" (New Spring, 1982).

9. Mark Galli, *Jesus Mean and Wild: The Unexpected Love of an Untamable God,* foreword by Eugene Peterson (Grand Rapids: Baker Books, 2006).

10. H. Richard Niebuhr, *The Kingdom of God in America* (New York, NY: Harper & Row, 1959), 193.

11. Karl Barth, *Church Dogmatics,* vol. 2, *The Doctrine of God* (Edinburgh: T&T Clark, 1957), 1:141.